THE TESTAMENT OF ADAM

SOCIETY
OF BIBLICAL
LITERATURE

DISSERTATION SERIES

edited by
Howard C. Kee
and
Douglas A. Knight

Number 52
THE TESTAMENT OF ADAM: AN EXAMINATION
OF THE SYRIAC AND GREEK TRADITIONS
by
Stephen Edward Robinson

Stephen Edward Robinson

THE TESTAMENT OF ADAM

AN EXAMINATION OF THE SYRIAC AND GREEK TRADITIONS

Scholars Press

Published by
Scholars Press
101 Salem Street
P.O. Box 2268
Chico, CA 95927

BS
1830
,T142
R62
1982

THE TESTAMENT OF ADAM
AN EXAMINATION OF THE
SYRIAC AND GREEK TRADITIONS

Stephen Edward Robinson

Ph.D., 1978
Duke University

Ph.D. Advisor:
James H. Charlesworth

Library of Congress Cataloging in Publication Data
Robinson, Stephen Edward.
  The Testament of Adam.
  (Dissertation series—Society of Biblical Literature ; no.
52; ISSN 0145–2770).
  Includes editions and translations of the Syriac and
Greek versions of the Testament of Adam (3 Syriac
recensions, the Greek version as far as extant, and
Georgios Cedrenos' paraphrase).
  Originally presented as the author's thesis, Duke, 1978.
  Bibliography: p.
  1. Testament of Adam—Criticism, interpretation, etc.
I. Testament of Adam (Greek version). II. Testament of
Adam (Syriac version). III. Title. IV. Series:Society of
Biblical Literature Dissertation series ; no. 52.
BS1830.T142R62 1980   229'.914   80–12209
ISBN 0–89130–399–5   AACR2

For Mom and Dad

TABLE OF CONTENTS

ACKNOWLEDGMENTS

I wish to express my deep appreciation to all of those who have helped in the preparation of this manuscript. I am especially indebted to Professor James H. Charlesworth under whose direction the research was conducted. He not only provided me with the initial idea for this study but also with invaluable advice in the course of its preparation. I wish also to express my appreciation to Professor Orval S. Wintermute, who is never too busy to see his students, and to Professors W. D. Davies, Roland E. Murphy, and John F. Oates for their pertinent suggestions.

Further thanks are due to the efficient staff of the Duke Divinity School Library and to Donn Michael Farris, the Divinity School Librarian. Mr. Emerson Ford is to be thanked for his efforts in the area of interlibrary loan.

I am especially grateful to the British Library, the John Rylands Library, the Bibliothèque Nationale and the Vatican Library for quickly and willingly supplying the photographs from which this edition of the text was taken. All the photographs for recension 1 (pp. 52-67) are courtesy of the British Library. The photographs of recensions 2 and 3 (pp. 68-101) are courtesy of the Vatican Library.

I wish to acknowledge the tremendous debt owed to my parents, Mr. and Mrs. Edward B. Robinson, who have throughout my life provided encouragement, support and a model of intellectual curiosity. Finally, I thank my wife, Janet, who is also my typist and without whose help this project could not have succeeded, and my children, Sarah, Becky, Emily and Michael, for their support.

S. E. R.

LIST OF ABBREVIATIONS

ANF   Roberts, A., and Donaldson, J., eds. *The Ante-Nicene Fathers*. 10 vols. Edinburgh: Clark, 1868-72; revised and reprinted, Grand Rapids, Mich.: Wm. B. Eerdmans Publishing Co., 1950-52.

APOT   Charles, R. H., ed. *The Apocrypha and Pseudepigrapha of the Old Testament*. 2 vols. Oxford: Clarendon Press, 1913.

AR   *Archiv für Religionswissenchaft*

AS   *American Scholar*

BJRL   *Bulletin of the John Rylands Library*

CBQ   *Catholic Biblical Quarterly*

HTR   *Harvard Theological Review*

JA   *Journal Asiatique*

JR   *Journal of Religion*

JSL   *Journal of Sacred Literature*

JTS   *Journal of Theological Studies*

LCL   Loeb Classical Library

NovT   *Novum Testamentum*

OCA   *Orientalia Christiana Analecta*

PG   Migne, J. P., ed. *Patrologia Graeca*. Paris: Garnier, 1894.

POT   Charlesworth, J. H., ed. *The Pseudepigrapha of the Old Testament*. Garden City: Doubleday, in press.

PS   Graffin, R., ed. *Patrologia Syriaca*. Paris: Firmin-Didot, 1907.

ROC   *Revue de l'Orient Chrétien*

RQ   *Revue de Qumran*

SHR   Studies in the History of Religion

SVTP   Studia in Veteris Testamenti Pseudepigrapha

TR	*Theologische Revue*
ZSVG	*Zeitschrift für Semitistik und verwandte Gebiete*
ZWT	*Zeitschrift für Wissenschaftliche Theologie*

INTRODUCTION

The last decade has witnessed a remarkable revival in the study of the Pseudepigrapha. This new interest has brought about the re-discovery of documents from the intertestamental period such as the Ladder of Jacob, the Treatise of Shem, and the Prayer of Jacob. Another fruitful area of study may lie in the reevaluation of documents which were examined and cast aside by an earlier generation of critics. Such a reexamination is demanded by the new perspectives on hellenistic Judaism, earliest Christianity and Gnosticism. Many documents deemed unworthy of serious study by scholars were disregarded because of a now outmoded methodology and an archaic critical perspective.

Such a document is the Testament of Adam. First treated in 1853, the Testament of Adam was the subject of a flurry of interest between 1890 and 1928, but the most important version, the Syriac, was never translated into English, and the testament has been the subject since that time of only one major article (encylopedic entries excluded). The reasons for this neglect can be attributed to the conclusions drawn by earlier critics that the testament was Gnostic or pagan in authorship, that it was merely a collection of unrelated fragments, and that it was of too late a date to warrant the interest of biblical scholarship.

As a result of this negative evaluation by earlier critics, the testament has been virtually ignored, if not completely forgotten. As recently as 1975, one meticulous and esteemed scholar could write a major book on early Syriac traditions without a reference to the Testament of Adam.[1]

The irony of this situation is, as we hope to show below, that the early critics were mistaken. The testament is neither Gnostic nor pagan; it is not a collection of fragments, but a coherent Syriac tradition which extends back to circa the third century A.D. in its Christian form, and utilizes Jewish sources

1

which apparently date much earlier. Certainly it is time to
take a fresh look at the Testament of Adam.

    In the study presented below, the Syriac and Greek ver-
sions of the testament receive primary attention. The Testament of Adam appears as an independent composition only in
Syriac and Arabic. The Arabic version is not treated here
since there is general agreement that it is dependent upon the
Syriac. Although our research indicates that the extant Greek
version is also dependent upon the Syriac, the Greek is very
important in discussing the original language and character of
the Testament of Adam. It is therefore necessary to treat both
the Syriac and the Greek versions. The translations offered
below are as literal as possible while maintaining good English.
This, of course, has caused the translation to be frequently
wooden. Hopefully the present study will help correct the
mistaken judgments of early critics and again place the Testament of Adam among the Pseudepigrapha of the Old Testament.

CHAPTER I
THE ADAM CYCLE OF JEWISH-CHRISTIAN LITERATURE

Prolegomena

The figure of Adam was long a favorite with the authors of both Jewish and Christian apocryphal and pseudepigraphical literature. As the first created one, the protoplast, Adam served as a revelator of the mysteries of creation and of the natural order of the universe. As the first human being, he stood as the archtypical exemplar of the human condition and of man in his quest for and relationship with God. As the mythical common ancestor, all human experience was conveniently subsumed under the experience of Adam in the beginning.[1] For this reason, the author of a canonical document, 1 Timothy, can seek to justify his view of the proper relationship between man and woman in marriage by an appeal to the relationship between Adam and Eve in the beginning.[2] The lives of our first parents obviously had normative significance in the mind of this early Christian writer. Jesus himself, in justifying so grave an irregularity as departure from the Mosaic tradition on the issue of divorce, chides the Pharisees with the fact that "from the beginning it was not so,"[3] thus appealing to man's original condition, the Adamic paradigm, in preference to the Mosaic.

It is precisely this paradigm inherent in the protoplast and the normative significance which was attributed to the traditions about Adam and Eve, together with a belief in the principle of τὰ ἐσχατὰ ὡς τὰ πρῶτα, that prompted Jews, Christians and Gnostics to appeal to the figure of Adam in support of their theological views. Thus, on the one hand, we see the author of 4 Ezra use Adam as a vehicle for his deterministic theology at 7:119:

> O thou Adam, what hast thou done! For though it was
> thou that sinned, the fall was not thine alone,
> but ours also who are thy descendants![4]

3

On the other hand, the author of 2 Baruch specifically contra-
dicts this idea by using a similar device at 54:15 and 19:

> For though Adam first sinned and brought untimely
> death upon all, yet of those who were born from
> him each one of them has prepared for his own soul
> torment to come, and again *each* one of them *has
> chosen* for himself glories to come . . . *Adam is*
> therefore *not the cause*, save only of his own soul,
> but *each of us has been the Adam of his own soul*.[5]
> (Italics mine)

G. H. Box felt that the contradiction between 2 Baruch and
4 Ezra was the result of two opposing apocalyptic schools, each
trying to gain control of the Adam traditions by pseudepigraphical means in order to further their own theological ends.[6]
Such normative significance attached to the figure of Adam
might be expected to produce a relatively large amount of traditional material about him, and to generate a correspondingly
large number of apocryphal and pseudepigraphical works attributed to him, and there is in fact a large body of Adam literature extending from the early intertestamental period well
into the Christian era. The immediate value of these pseudepigraphical works lies in the light they shed on the religious
orientations of their various authors. As J. B. Frey expressed
it,

> Si ces légendes n'ajoutent rien à notre science
> des origines, elles nous permettent du moins de
> connaître les idées de leurs auteurs et, à ce point
> de vue, elles ont leur importance.[7]

The Books of Adam

The expansion of the Adam tradition had already begun in
early Hellenistic times with the Book of Jubilees, among others,
and continued in Judaism with the writings of Philo and
Josephus, with 4 Ezra, 2 Baruch, the Apocalypse of Moses and
the *Vita Adae et Evae*. These Jewish works were followed by
such Christian compositions as the Cave of Treasures and the
Combat of Adam and Eve. We find in use among the Gnostics
books such as the Apocalypse of Adam and the Gospel of Eve.
Set against this background of Jewish, Christian and Gnostic
Adam traditions is a little-known pseudepigraphon entitled the
Testament of Adam, which is extant in numerous recensions and

languages.[8] The Testament of Adam is often found incorporated
into later works, such as the Arabic (but not the Syriac) Cave
of Treasures or Book of the Rolls; but, as we will show below,
it is both independent of and prior to them.

Since the Testament of Adam has often been confused with
other books of the Adam cycle, it is pertinent here to review
briefly the references to books of Adam in ancient sources and
also the extant documents which are attributed to Adam.

The Book of Adam

Specific references to books attributed to Adam are frequent in antiquity. The Apostolic Constitutions warn Christian
readers of several heretical books, among them a Book of Adam:

> And among the ancients also some have written
> apocryphal books of Moses, and Enoch, and Adam,
> and Isaiah, and David, and Elijah, and of the
> three patriarchs, pernicious and repugnant to the
> truth.[9]

Rabbinic evidence for a Book of Adam is vague, although
there is a wealth of traditional material about Adam in rabbinic
literature. L. Zunz believed that the existence of an actual
Book of Adam was indicated by the following passages:[10]

> Abodah Zara 5a. But did not Resh Lakish [himself]
> say, What is the meaning of the verse *This is the
> book of the generations of Adam*? Did Adam have a
> book? What it implies is that the Holy One, blessed
> be he, showed to Adam every [coming] generation with
> its expositors, every generation with its sages,
> every generation with its leaders; when he reached
> the generation of R. Akiba he rejoiced at his teach-
> ing, but was grieved about his death, and said, *How
> precious are Thy thoughts unto me, O God!*[11]

> Genesis Rabbah 24:2. While Adam lay a shapeless
> mass before Him at whose decree the world came into
> existence, He showed him every generation and its
> Sages, every generation and its judges, scribes,
> interpreters, and leaders. Said He to him: "Thine
> eyes did see unformed substance: the unformed sub-
> stances [viz. thy potential descendants] which thine
> eyes did see have already been written in the book
> of Adam": viz. THIS IS THE BOOK OF THE GENERATIONS
> OF ADAM.[12]

There is a further reference to a book of Adam at Exodus Rabbah
40:2:

God did not, however, tell Moses whom he should
appoint, hence Moses inquired: "To whom shall I
speak?" God replied: "I will show thee." So what
did the Holy One, blessed be He, do? He brought
him the book of Adam and showed him all the gener-
ations that would arise from Creation to Resurrec-
tion, each generation and its kings, its leaders,
and its prophets, saying unto him: "I have appointed
all these [for their destinies] from that time
[Creation], and Bezalel, too, I have appointed from
that time."[13]

and another at Baba Mezia 85b-86a:

Samuel Yarhina'ah was Rabbi's physician. Now,
Rabbi having contracted an eye disease, Samuel
offered to bathe it with a lotion, but he said,
"I cannot bear it." "Then I will apply an ointment
to it," he said. "This too I cannot bear," he
objected. So he placed a phial of chemicals under
his pillow, and he was healed. Rabbi was most
anxious to ordain him, but the opportunity was
lacking. Let it not grieve thee, he said; I have
seen the Book of Adam, in which is written,
"Samuel Yarhina'ah [86a] shall be called "Sage",
but not "Rabbi", and Rabbi's healing shall come
through him.[14]

L. Ginzberg insisted that Zunz was in error, and that
while a Jewish book of Adam must have been in existence perhaps
as early as the first century, it is never referred to in the
Talmud.[15] The references cited above are indeed ambiguous,
for the books of Adam referred to may be the Book of Genesis,
or perhaps a mystical book in God's possession out of which
revelations were vouchsafed to certain sages. None of these
passages necessarily refers to a Book of Adam extant in Jewish
circles in intertestamental times. However, while Ginzberg
denies that the Talmud ever refers to a Book of Adam, he does
maintain that the cycle of Adam literature as a whole "can
only be explained by the Midrash. The legends of Adam with
which rabbinic literature abounds seems to point to the same
source."[16]

In the so-called list of "Sixty Books" appended in some
manuscripts to the Questions and Responses of Anastasius of
Sinai, a Book of Adam stands at the head of the apocryphal
books of the Old Testament:

Book of Adam
Book of Enoch
Book of Lamech
Book of the Patriarchs

Prayer of Joseph
Eldad and Modad
Testament of Moses
Assumption of Moses
Psalms of Solomon
Apocalypse of Elias
Vision of Esaias
Apocalypse of Sophonias
Apocalypse of Zacharias
Apocalypse of Esdras[17]

At the close of the thirteenth century, Mechithar of
Airivank formulated a further list of apocryphal books, and as
in the "Sixty Books", a Book of Adam stands at the head of the
list:

These are the books which the Jews have in Secret
Of Adam,
Of Enoch,
Of the Sibyl,
The XII Patriarchs,
The Prayer of Joseph,
The Assumption of Moses,
Eldad and Modad,
The Psalms of Solomon,
The Apocrypha (or: Hidden Things) of Elijah,
The Seventh Vision of Daniel[18]

One of the Armenian books of Adam published in 1896 has
often been referred to as the Book of Adam.[19] This work is
actually an Armenian version of the Life of Adam and Eve, or
more specifically, the Apocalypse of Moses. The title "The
Book of Adam" appears to have been added in the Armenian version, and the original title is now the first line of the text:
"This is the life of Adam and Eve."[20] This work should not be
referred to as the Book of Adam, but rather as the Armenian
Life of Adam and Eve. However, this text does establish that
the Life of Adam and Eve was known in some circles as the Book
of Adam.

Finally, modern critics have sometimes used the title "The
Book of Adam" to refer to any of several books of the Adam
cycle, singly or in combination. This practice is a result of
the now discredited hypothesis that there was in antiquity
only one book of Adam which was known by several different
titles. The resulting equation of very non-equivalent documents
has given birth to many misconceptions about specific books and
about the Adam literature generally.[21] The specific title "The
Book of Adam" should never be used in this generic sense.

Testament of the Protoplasts

Although the attribution of the "Sixty Books" to Anastasius of Sinai is disputed, there is no question that he wrote
the following short notice in his commentary on the Hexaemeron:

> The Jews on the authority of a book which is not in
> the canon and which is called the Testament of the
> Protoplasts affirm that Adam entered Paradise on the
> fourth day.[22]

This is the only reference in antiquity to this work. It is
the opinion of J. B. Frey that this is a reference to the Life
of Adam and Eve.[23]

The Apocalypse of Adam

In the writings of the Church Fathers there is very little
indication that an Adam book was extant in the early Church.
The only patristic reference to such a work is that of Epiphanius, who mentions that "apocalypses of Adam" were current
among the Gnostics.[24]

In 1945 an Apocalypse of Adam (CG V, 5) was discovered
among the codices of the Nag Hammadi Library, and has been
edited by A. Böhlig and P. Labib.[25] This document has close
affinities with the Testament of Adam and with the Jewish
traditions about Adam and Seth cited by Josephus.[26] There is
general agreement that the work is non-Christian, and originally Jewish in character, although in its final form it is
certainly Gnostic. The Apocalypse of Adam purports to contain
a revelation given by Adam to Seth concerning the mysteries of
salvation, the future of the world and the coming of an
Illuminator.[27]

But the Apocalypse of Adam was not confined to use among
the Gnostics. Note, for example, the Epistle of Barnabas 2:10:

> To us then he speaks thus: "Sacrifice for the
> Lord is a broken heart, a smell of sweet savour
> to the Lord is a heart that glorifieth him that
> made it."[28]

The first clause comes from Psalm 51:17; the second clause is
unknown, although the entire passage is quoted in the same form
by both Irenaeus and Clement of Alexandria.[29] The Constantinople manuscript of the Epistle of Barnabus identifies this
unknown clause with the marginal note: "Psalm 50 (51) and in

the Apocalypse of Adam."[30] It was the judgment of M. R. James
that the source of all three patristic quotations was an apocryphal Apocalypse of Adam.[31] If so, there must have been at
least two apocalypses as the notice in Epiphanius indicates,
for the passage is not found in the Coptic Apocalypse of Adam.

The Penitence of Adam

In the Latin list of apocryphal books known as the Gelasian
Decree there is mention of two books connected with Adam. The
Gelasian Decree has generally been attributed to Pope Gelasius
I (496), although some manuscripts attribute it to Damasus
(384) and some to Hormisdas (523). E. von Dobschütz, however,
maintains that the Decree is a French compilation of the sixth
century.[32] That part of the list which concerns us is as
follows:

§ 4.7	Liber de filiabus Adae Leptogeneseos	apocryphus
6.2	Liber qui appellatur Paenitentia Adae	apocryphus
6.3	Liber de Ogia nomine gigante qui post diluvium cum dracone ab haereticis pugnasse perhibetur	apocryphus
6.4	Liber qui appellatur Testamentum Iob	apocryphus
6.7	Liber qui appellatur Paenitentia Iamne et Mambre	apocryphus
8.5	Scriptura quae appellatur Salmonis Interdictio	apocrypha
8.6	Phylacteria omnia quae non angelorum, ut illi confingunt, sed daemonum magis nominibus conscripta sunt[33]	apocrypha

A History of the Penitence of Adam and Eve, which borrows
heavily from the Life of Adam and Eve, is found among the Armenian Adam books. This makes the identification of the Penitence
of Adam with the Life of Adam and Eve, which has been suggested
by some scholars, a tempting idea. However, the Armenian Penitence, though dependent upon the Life of Adam and Eve, differs
with it at many points and should, therefore, be granted separate consideration. Since the Gelasian Decree offers no sample
passage from its Penitence, it cannot be established for certain
that the Armenian Penitence is the same document.

Toward the end of the twelfth century Samuel of Ani
recorded a list of books which had been brought into Armenia
and translated into the language of that country about A.D. 590
by Nestorian Christians from Syria:

                    Kaurdosag
                    Guiragosag

> Vision of St. Paul
> Repentance of Adam
> Testament [sic]
> Infancy of the Lord
> Sebios
> Cluster of Blessing
> The Book Which Ought Not to be Hid
> Exposition of the Gospel of Mani[34]

The name of Adam would seem to belong to both the Repentance
and Testament in Samuel's list. If this is so, his list is
valuable evidence for the existence of both a Penitence *and*
a Testament of Adam.

The Book of the Daughters of Adam, the Little Genesis

Besides the Penitence of Adam, the Gelasian Decree also
mentions a Book of the Daughters of Adam, the Little Genesis.
J. A. Hort and R. H. Charles interpret the citation as an indication that the Book of the Daughters of Adam consisted of
excerpts from the Book of Jubilees which is often called the
Little Genesis.[35] On the other hand, E. Schürer and J. B. Frey
insist that the Book of the Daughters of Adam was mistakenly
associated with the Little Genesis by the author of the Gelasian
Decree.[36] They judge that the Book of the Daughters of Adam
would be an inappropriate title for the Book of Jubilees. If
the two were indeed separate works, the Book of the Daughters
of Adam is now lost. The Book of Jubilees itself should not be
considered part of the Adam cycle since Adam is only a peripheral character and his story is outside the main thrust of
the work.

The Life of Adam

The Byzantine chronicler George Syncellus (c. A.D. 800)
twice refers to a "so-called Life of Adam." These references
are all that is known about the work.[37] Syncellus may be
referring to the Life of Adam and Eve, a possibility suggested
by the similarity of the two titles, but unless more evidence
is forthcoming to support this hypothesis, the Life of Adam
should be treated as a separate work, since Syncellus' short
synopsis seems incompatible with the contents of the extant
Life of Adam and Eve.

The Life of Adam and Eve (Apocalypse of Moses)

Perhaps the most important of the books of Adam in terms
of influence upon other works are the two recensions of the
Life of Adam and Eve, the Latin *Vita Adae et Evae* and the Greek
Apocalypse of Moses. The *Vita* has been edited by W. Meyer[38]
and the Apocalypse of Moses by C. Tischendorf.[39] This work is
an haggadic midrash on the life of Adam and Eve after their
expulsion from Eden. The *Vita*, but not the Apocalypse, contains an account of the penitence of Adam and Eve after the
Fall. However, the impulse to equate this document with the
Penitence of Adam should be resisted.

The Cave of Treasures

The Syriac text of the Cave of Treasures was first published by C. Bezold in 1888, following a German translation
which appeared in 1883.[40] An English translation was published
by E. A. W. Budge in 1927.[41] Portions of the Cave of Treasures
appear in Arabic, Karshuni, Ethiopic, Old Georgian, and Armenian as parts of a pseudo-Clementine work usually called the
Book of the Rolls.[42]

The Cave of Treasures relates the succession of families
from Adam to Christ with emphasis on the burial of Adam and
the eventual placement of his body on the hill at Golgotha.
The Cave of Treasures has been dated anywhere from the second
to the sixth centuries A.D., but a date in the fourth century
seems most likely for its final redaction, although it doubt-
less uses sources that are much earlier.[43] The Cave of Treasures is of particular importance to the study of the Testament
of Adam because of the often recurring but incorrect assertion
that the latter is literarily dependent on the former.

The Conflict of Adam and Eve with Satan

The Conflict of Adam and Eve with Satan was first made
known by A. Dillmann in 1853, when he translated the work into
German from Ethiopic.[44] It was translated into English in 1882
by S. C. Malan.[45] There is general agreement that it is a
late Christian composition and is dependent upon both the Life
of Adam and Eve and the Cave of Treasures. The Conflict is
divided into three parts, the actual struggle of Adam and Eve
with Satan after leaving the Garden of Eden, the history of the

patriarchs down to Melchizedek, and the history of Israel down
to the birth of Jesus at Bethlehem.

The Armenian Adam Books

In 1896 H. S. Josepheanz first published the Armenian
books of Adam. This was followed in 1901 by the English translation of J. Issaverdens. These consist of eight short but
separate works which appear to have been translated into
Armenian from Greek. With the exception of the Armenian Life
of Adam and Eve, and the History of the Penitence of Adam and
Eve, which have been discussed above, each book is amply des-
cribed by its title:

> The Book of Adam [The Armenian Life of Adam and Eve]
> History of the Creation and of the Transgression of
>   Adam
> History of the Expulsion of Adam from the Garden
> History of Cain and Abel, the Sons of Adam
> The Promise of Seth, to Which We Must Give Ear
> History of the Penitence of Adam and Eve
> Adam's Words to Seth
> The Death of Adam[46]

This important group of pseudepigrapha, like the Testament of
Adam, has not received the attention it deserves, although
research in this area has recently been undertaken by M. Stone.

The Testament of Adam

The testimony of Samuel of Ani concerning this document
has already been cited above (p. 9). Samuel listed a Testament
(of Adam) among the apocryphal books which were brought into
Armenia by Nestorian Christians in A.D. 590. The earliest citation from the Testament of Adam is found in the Syriac (but not
the Greek) *Transitus Mariae*, a document generally dated in the
fourth or fifth century A.D. A. Smith Lewis has edited and
translated a Syriac manuscript of the *Transitus Mariae* which
dates from the fifth century and contains the following statement:

> And the Magi came and brought the offerings, and they
> brought the testament of Adam with them. And from
> the testament of Adam all mankind have learned to
> make testaments; and from the Messiah, who was born
> of Mary, all mankind who were in darkness, have been
> enlightened. And thus from Adam to Seth writing was
> used; and from Seth letters were written, to the
> fathers and to all mankind; and the fathers gave

[them] to the sons' sons; and they said that "The
Messiah shall come, and shall be born of Mary the
Virgin in Bethlehem."[47]

The next citation taken from the Testament of Adam is
found in the writings of the Byzantine historian and collector,
George Cedrenus.[48] He writes:

> Adam, in the six hundredth year, having repented,
> learned by revelation the things concerning the
> Watchers and the Flood, and about repentance and the
> divine Incarnation, and about the prayers that are
> sent up to God by all creatures at each hour of
> the day and night, with the help of Uriel, the
> archangel over repentance. Thus, in the first hour
> of the day the first prayer is completed in heaven;
> in the second, the prayer of angels; in the third,
> the prayer of winged things; in the fourth, the
> prayer of domestic animals; in the fifth, the
> prayer of wild beasts; in the sixth, the review of
> the angels and the inspection of all creation; in
> the seventh, the entrance of the angels to God and
> the exit of the angels; in the eighth, the praise
> and sacrifices of the angels; in the ninth, the
> petition and worship of men; in the tenth, the
> visitations of the waters and the petition of the
> heavenly and earthly beings; in the eleventh, the
> thanksgiving and rejoicing of all things; in the
> twelfth, the entreaty of human beings for favor.[49]

This list of the hours of the day and night, or Horarium, is
clearly that found in our Testament of Adam.[50] M. R. James
concluded on the basis of the penitence mentioned in this
passage that the Testament of Adam originally contained an
account of Adam's repentance as well as the Horarium found here.
It must be noted, however, that while the passage contains elements which can be so interpreted, Cedrenus cites no reference
and may be speaking generally of traditions known to him, con-
flating elements from both a Penitence and a Testament of Adam.

The possibility that the Latin Church knew the Testament
of Adam is presented by a citation from *de Psalmodiae Bono* 3,
by Nicetas of Remesiana. In manuscripts A and V of that work
we find the following:

> Neque enim illud volumen termerarie recipiendum est
> cuius inscriptio est INQUISITIO ABRAHAE ubi cantasse
> ipsa animalia et fontes et elementa finguntur. Cum
> nullius sit fidei liber ipse nulla auctoritate
> subnixus.[51]

M. R. James has suggested that since the title *Inquisitio
Abrahae* occurs nowhere else, and since the description of the

contents of that work agrees so well with the contents of the
Horarium from the Testament of Adam, that the title *Inquisitio
Abrahae* should be emended to *Dispositio Adae*, i.e. the Testament of Adam.[52] His suggestion was rejected by Frey and
Schürer.[53] However, *dispositio* is a legitimate rendering of
διαθήκη, and one of the earliest and perhaps the best manuscript of *de Psalmodiae Bono*, manuscript A, attributes the
Inquisitio to Abrae, rather than Abrahae.[54] The confusion of
Abrae with Adae was an easy mistake to make. In an inscription
from Podgoritza, the artist
has made this same error.
Evidently he began to label
the panel which contained the
figures of Adam and Eve "Abram
et fili", but half-way through
realized his error and added
Eve's name.[55] Considering
the similarity between
inquisitio and *dispositio*,
and the ease with which Abram
could be confused with Adam,
James' suggestion should be
allowed to stand, if only as a possibility.

     Another work entitled A Narrative Concerning the Expulsion
of Adam is contained in the Codex Athos Vatopedi 84 (formerly
79).[56] However, this work should not be included in our Adam-
cycle since, as Denis points out, it is in reality an exerpt
from the homily on Genesis 3 attributed to St. John Chrysos-
tom.[57]

     The tradition of a testament given by Adam to his son Seth
concerning the future of the world and the advent of a great
prophet is found in Islamic literature in both the Annals of
Tabari[58] and in a work entitled *de generatione Machumet et
nutritia eius*.[59] In both passages the prophecy spoken by Adam
is meant to refer to the advent of Mohammed rather than that
of Christ.

     As late as 1615 G. Gualmyn in his commentary on M. Psellus'
de Daemonum Operatione, quoted a fragment of the Horarium from
the Testament of Adam found in a Paris magical codex attributed
falsely to Apollonius of Tyana.[60]

By way of summary then, the books of Adam mentioned in the
ancient sources are:

> The Book of Adam (Apostolic Constitutions,
> Sixty Books, Mechithar of Airivank)
> The Testament of the Protoplasts (Anastasius
> of Sinai)
> The Apocalypse of Adam (Epiphanius, Epistle
> of Barnabas)
> The Penitence of Adam (Gelasian Decree, Samuel
> of Ani)
> The Book of the Daughters of Adam, The Little
> Genesis (Gelasian Decree)
> The Life of Adam (George Syncellus)
> The Testament of Adam (Samuel of Ani, George
> Cedrenus, *Transitus Mariae*, Nicetas of
> Remesiana, *de generatione Machumet*,
> Tabari, Gilbert Gualmyn)

The extant books of Adam are:

> The Apocalypse of Adam
> The Testament of Adam
> The Life of Adam and Eve (Apocalypse of Moses
> and *Vita Adae et Evae*)
> The Cave of Treasures
> The Conflict of Adam and Eve with Satan
> The Armenian Adam Books:
> > The Book of Adam (The Armenian Life of Adam
> > and Eve)
> > History of the Creation and of the Trans-
> > gression of Adam
> > History of the Expulsion of Adam from the
> > garden
> > History of Cain and Abel, the Sons of Adam
> > The Promise of Seth, to Which We Must Give Ear
> > History of the Penitence of Adam and Eve
> > Adam's Words to Seth
> > The Death of Adam

Obviously, the two lists do not match. Nor should we
expect them to, given the random nature of the historical acci-
dent which may preserve an entire text, or merely a reference
to it, or may preserve of it nothing at all. It would be
unreasonable to expect that the few documents which have survived are precisely those documents which are mentioned in the
ancient sources. And yet the impulse to "tidy up" by making
forced equations seems to be for many scholars an irresistible
siren. It has been suggested, for example, that the Penitence
of Adam mentioned in the Gelasian Decree should be identified
with the Life of Adam and Eve merely because both works deal
with the theme of Adam's repentance. Several scholars have
suggested that the Penitence, Apocalypse and Testament of Adam

must be the same document under different names.[61] The evaluation of M. R. James is typical: "The testament of Adam,
otherwise called the Apocalypse, or Penitence of Adam, or Apocalypse of Moses."[62] In his article on the Adam material for
Cheyne's *Encyclopedia Biblica*, James makes the further equation:

> Testament (or Apocalypse, or Penitence) of Adam:
> Book of the Conflict of Adam and Eve.--Extant
> partially in Greek, Latin, Syriac, Arabic, Ethiopic
> [and Coptic].
>
> These versions represent variously developed forms
> or fragments of a Jewish romance dealing with the
> life of Adam and Eve after the Fall, and with their
> death and burial. We no longer possess the romance
> in its original form.[63]

Despite James' evaluation, there is no evidence that these
books were ever part of the same document. Nor is there any
justification for combining two or three titles known from
ancient sources and applying them indiscriminately to a single
extant document. This kind of Procrustean approach to the
Apocrypha and Pseudepigrapha is surely ill-advised and moti-
vated by the impulse to match every reference with an extant
book. Some of the documents may have circulated under different titles, but that possiblity can only be established by
literary comparison and not by guesswork about the contents of
lost books. To the present, all attempts to equate the Testament and Penitence of Adam have ignored the testimony of Samuel
of Ani that the Penitence and Testament known to him were two
separate documents. Furthermore, the discovery of an Apocalypse of Adam among the codices of the Nag Hammadi Library[64]
which is markedly different from the extant testament offers a
further caution against too facilely equating different titles.
The casual use of inexact titles in reference to the books of
Adam is no longer acceptable. It is far more likely that
instead of a single Adam book, we are dealing with a whole
cycle of Adam literature originating in the intertestamental
period and continuing to expand well into the Christian era.[65]
It is to this cycle of Adam literature that our Testament of
Adam belongs, one of many independent and often contradictory
documents.

A Description of the Testament of Adam

The Testament of Adam is witnessed primarily by several
Syriac texts which E. Renan, the first scholar to work on them,
divided into four sections. The first section is a list of the
hours of the night together with that portion of God's creation
which renders praises to God at each hour. The second section
consists of a similar catalog of the hours of the day and the
creatures which render praises at each hour. The third section
is a collection of prophecies which Adam delivers to his posterity, primarily to Seth, concerning the future of the world
and of the human race. Adam foretells the flood; the birth,
passion and death of Christ; and the final end of the world.
This section ends with the statement of Seth that he has
recorded the testament of his father Adam, and buried it in the
cave of treasures.

The fourth section is an account of the different orders
of heavenly beings: angels, archangels, powers, principalities,
etc. This section has nothing in it to identify it with the
Adam literature, and the majority of scholars believe that its
inclusion in the Testament of Adam is due to a scribal error,
since it appears in only one manuscript of the testament. However, a careful examination reveals that while this section was
not a part of the original testament, its inclusion in Vatican
Syriac manuscript 164 constitutes an intentional addition to the
text rather than a scribal error.[66] This fourth section contains references to the prophet Zechariah, the defeat of Sennacherib, and to the victories of Judah the Maccabee.

Beginning with M. Kmosko,[67] the Testament of Adam has
usually been divided into three parts rather than Renan's four.
These sections are the Horarium or hours of the day and night,
the Prophecy, and the Hierarchy. We shall follow the practice
of Kmosko, Frey and others in using the terms Horarium, Prophecy, and Hierarchy to refer to the three sections of the Testament of Adam.

The Testament of Adam is extant in Syriac, Greek, Arabic,
Karshuni, Ethiopic, Old Georgian and Armenian. However, it is
found as an *independent* composition only in Syriac and Arabic.
In Arabic, Ethiopic, Old Georgian and Armenian it is also found
within a section of the later Christian work called the Cave of

Treasures. This section of the Cave of Treasures has itself
been incorporated into a larger and still later work which is
variously titled the Book of the Rolls, the Book of the Mysteries of Heaven and Earth, or the Apocalypse of Peter.[68]

The following relationships should be made clear at this
point. First, the Syriac Testament of Adam is a self-contained
and independent composition. Despite frequent assertions to
the contrary, it does not appear as part of the Syriac Cave of
Treasures, nor is there any evidence that it ever did.[69] The
Testament of Adam and the Cave of Treasures are found on the
same manuscript twice, but are separated by totally extraneous
matter.[70] Second, references which state that the Testament of
Adam appears in the Arabic version of the Cave of Treasures are
misleading, since the Cave of Treasures does not occur in Arabic
as a self-contained text.[71] These Arabic manuscripts actually
combine the Testament of Adam with a major portion of the Cave
of Treasures to form the larger Book of the Rolls, which is
attributed to Clement of Rome, and ultimately to the Apostle
Peter. For this reason, it will be referred to below as a
"pseudo-Clementine" work. Third, what is true of the Arabic is
true also of the Karshuni and Ethiopic versions: the Testament
of Adam does not appear either by itself or with the Cave of
Treasures apart from the context of the pseudo-Clementine work.
Fourth, whenever the Testament of Adam appears in the Arabic
Book of the Rolls, it is clearly labelled "The Testament of
Adam."[72]

The Greek version of the testament consists solely of the
Horarium, and is found in two forms. The first is the portion
of the Horarium quoted by George Cedrenus (11th century); the
second incorporates the Horarium into a Byzantine text which
emphasizes the magical significance of the names provided in
the Greek manuscripts for each of the hours. This is in contrast with the Syriac version where the emphasis is upon the
unity of God's creation in rendering praises to him; but the
practice is in keeping with the high esteem given Hebrew cosmological ideas in Byzantine magical texts.

CHAPTER II

FROM ASSEMANI TO REININK: THE TESTAMENT
AND ITS CRITICS

History of Critical Study

Modern critical study of the Testament of Adam began with
J. S. Assemani's discovery of a manuscript in the Oriental
Library of the Vatican which he called: "Otiosi cujusdam Syri
putidum opus."[1] His unflattering announcement drew little
attention until 1853, when E. Renan published an article on the
testament with a Syriac text and a French translation.[2] Renan
took his text from two Vatican Syrïac manuscripts, 58 and 164,
and from four Arabic manuscripts; one from the Vatican, Arabo
32, and three from the Bibliothèque impériale, arabe 52, 54,
and 158. After his article was completed, he compared his text
against the British Museum Additional manuscript 14,624, and,
deciding that the latter was identical with Vatican manuscript
58, he did not use it.

Renan believed the Testament of Adam to be a fragment of
a Gnostic work which was popular in the early centuries of the
Christian era. He suggested that this single Gnostic work was
responsible for all the various references to books of Adam
found in the ancient sources known to him. In 1853, this suggestion was not as unreasonable as it might seem today, since
the Testament of Adam was the only book of Adam extant at that
time.[3] However, to shore up his equation of all the different
titles known to him from antiquity with a single extant document, Renan claimed that the terms μετάνοια (from the Penitence
of Adam) and ἀποκάλυψις (from the Apocalypse of Adam) were
interchangeable synonyms in apocalyptic literature. Noting
that Samuel of Ani listed *both* a Penitence and a Testament in
his list, Renan dismissed the fact with the following argument:

> Mais, d'une part, nous avons établi que la *Pénitence*
> et l'*Apocalypse d'Adam* n'étaient qu'un même livre.
> [i.e., by the unsupported claim that μετάνοια and
> ἀποκάλυψις are synonymous terms.] De l'autre, les

> fragments donnés par Cédrénus comme extraits de
> l'*Apocalypse*, se retrouvent presque mot pour mot
> dans les manuscrits syriaques et arabes, sous le
> titre de *Testament d'Adam*.[4]

But Cedrenus had not, in fact, identified his material as coming
from an Apocalypse of Adam. A careful reading of the text
clearly shows that Cedrenus gives no references whatsoever for
the material he quotes.[5] The aorist participle μετανόησας used
by Cedrenus reveals only that Adam's repentance occurred prior
to the action represented in the quotation, while the anarthrous
noun ἀποκαλύψεως indicates that Adam received knowledge not
"from the Apocalypse," but rather "through revelation."[6] The
close juxtaposition of a cognate of μετάνοια with a form of
ἀποκάλυψις in Cedrenus' text hardly justifies the identification of such a dual-titled work as his source.[7] The themes of
repentance and revelation are an integral part of the traditions concerning Adam generally. Their occurrence together,
even close together, would not be surprising or out of place in
any apocryphal book attributed to Adam.

Renan suggested that the use of the canonical hours in the
early Christian Church might be derived from the hours in the
first part of the Testament of Adam. Unfortunately, he offered
no evidence for this opinion other than the concern of both
with the hours of the day and night. In addition, Renan was
also the first critic to attribute the third section of the
testament, the Hierarchy, to pseudo-Dionysius the Areopagite.

Renan listed several reasons for attributing the Testament
of Adam to Gnostic authorship. He alluded to, but did not cite
examples of, parallels between the Testament of Adam and the
Persian Avesta. Renan pictured Persian ideas entering into
Christian Gnosticism through the medium of the Mandaeans, whom
he equated with the Elkasaites.[8] He believed that the significance of the role of Seth in the Testament of Adam was a clear
indication that the work was closely related to Sethian Gnostics.
The mention of ablutions, a preoccupation with astrology, the
use of angels as revelators, the attribution of magical power
to the elements, and even the attribution of the book to an
antediluvian figure were all seen by Renan as evidence for a
Gnostic origin of the Testament of Adam.[9]

In his evaluation of the Gnostic character of the work,
Renan was clearly handicapped by an archaic conception of the
nature of Gnosticism and of intertestamental Judaism. Although
his initial judgments were formed in an almost complete vacuum
of primary sources, they have been followed by some scholars up
to the present time. The attribution of the Testament of Adam
to the Gnostics has been most particularly and uncritically persistent, and has contributed greatly to the neglect shown the
document by later scholars.[10]

In 1877, J. A. Hort treated the Testament of Adam briefly
in his article for the *Dictionary of Christian Biography*.[11]
Hort shared with Renan the belief that the Testament of Adam
was early and that it was the single document responsible for
all the references to books of Adam in the ancient sources:
"These fragments evidently represent a work current under different titles in the early ages."[12] Hort, like Renan, noted
the testimony of Samuel of Ani that there were two separate
works, a Penitence and a Testament, and like Renan, he also
dismissed it: "Yet, if as appears likely, Adam's name belongs
to both titles, the nature of the existing fragments is not
such as to compel us to suppose that they designate two wholly
distinct books."[13] It is at once obvious that Hort's argument
assumes the extant fragments of the Testament of Adam to be
derived from the documents cited by Samuel of Ani, an assumption
for which there is no proof. Second, Hort's argument is based
not on the ancient citation in question but on the nature of the
extant fragments--in short Samuel's testimony has been ignored.
Hort agreed with Renan that the juxtaposition of the words
repentance and revelation in the passage from Cedrenus indicated
dual titles for the same work: "and it is to be observed that
'repentance' and 'revelation' are prominent words, while 'testament' holds a yet more significant place in the Syriac prophecy.
Thus the three names are brought together."[14]

Although Hort concluded that all of the fragments known to
him were from a single work and that the Horarium and the Prophecy of Adam to Seth were particularly closely related, he
entertained the notion that the fourth fragment which he called
the Heavenly Hierarchy was a later appendix to the work. His
notice of the disparate character of one of the fragments would

be amplified by later scholars who would incorrectly conclude
that the fragments of the Testament of Adam were not a unity.

One lasting influence of Hort's treatment was the suggestion that the Testament of Adam was related to the Cave of
Treasures and to the Conflict of Adam and Eve with Satan. This
identification of the Testament with the Cave of Treasures,
while not strictly intended by Hort, may have encouraged later
scholars to treat the Testament as part of the Cave of Treasures rather than as a self-contained work. The eventual result
of this trend was that the Testament was subsequently dated
with the Cave of Treasures and was classified as a late Christian work.

Hort did not share the rather antagonistic viewpoint of
Assemani and Renan concerning the character of the Testament of
Adam,[15] but was in fact quite impressed with the document. He
wrote: "The Testament, as it stands, is short and unpretend-
ing: yet a lofty spirit pervades a great part of it." Hort
also rejected as groundless Renan's claim of Gnostic origins
for the Testament of Adam. He attributed the Horarium and the
other cosmological elements of the testament not to Gnostic
speculation, but to the desire of the author to represent "the
community of all created things." Hort maintained that although
the testament was not a product of Latin or Greek Christianity,
it should not therefore automatically be classified as a product of Gnosticism but rather as "an interesting monument of
an almost unknown world of ancient creeds."[16]

The indefatigable M. R. James added a great deal of manuscript evidence to the study of the Testament of Adam, locating
several previously unknown references to Adam literature in
general and to the Testament of Adam in particular. In 1892,
in an article on the Testament of Abraham, James was the first
to note the existence of the Greek fragments of the Testament
of Adam found in the Paris magical codex 2419, and also the
quotations from that codex by Gilbert Gualmyn in his edition of
Michael Psellus' *de Daemonum Operatione*.[17] James was also the
first to cite the marginal note from the Constantinople manuscript of the Epistle of Barnabas, which mentions the Apocalypse
of Adam, also pointing out that the same passage was quoted by
Irenaeus and Clement of Alexandria.[18] In addition to these

discoveries James suggested that the passage from Nicetas of
Remesiana was a possible Latin version of the Testament of
Adam,[19] and also improved upon Hort's observation of a disparity
between the extant fragments of the testament by recognizing
(correctly) that the fourth fragment was not part of the Adam
tradition at all, and concluding (incorrectly) that it had been
mislabelled by a scribe.[20]

James originally had believed with Renan and Hort that
there was only one book of Adam in antiquity, and that it had
been known by several different names. However, over a period
of thirty years he changed his mind, deciding in the face of
greater and greater variation in the ever more plentiful sources
that there must have been at least two separate books. He
revised and softened his original position that the Apocalypse,
Penitence, and Testament of Adam must be the same document,
saying instead that "There is thus a prima facie case for thinking that the *Apocalypse*, *Penitence*, and *Testament of Adam*, if
not identical, at least contained a good deal of common
matter."[21]

James' conclusion, finally, was that the Testament of
Adam, although originally a Jewish document, had become hope-
lessly Christianized.

> If the horary and the prophecy were parts of the
> same book, it was a Christian, or at least a fully
> Christianized text, and not a very early one. Yet
> I find it difficult not to suspect the existence
> of an early book behind it.[22]

Thus, while James rightly had begun to see that the sources of
the Adam tradition were not homogenous, he also gave added
impetus to the misconception inadvertently created by Hort that
the testament was a late Christian composition. James maintained that the mention of a "cave of treasures" in the Testament of Adam indicated a similarity between the latter document
and a whole series of late Christian compositions. As a result,
the classification of the Testament of Adam as a late Christian
work was to become firmly entrenched through its supposed
association with other late Christian works, particularly with
the Syriac Cave of Treasures.

In 1906 C. Bezold published an eclectic edition of the
Arabic and Ethiopic texts of the Testament of Adam in the

T. Nöldeke Festschrift.[23] It was these texts that E. A. W.
Budge used for his English translation of the testament.[24]
Bezold labelled the testament a "Gnostic tractate" which he
believed had been inserted into the Arabic version of the Cave
of Treasures and had from thence passed into the Ethiopic version. He offers no evidence in support of his attribution of
Gnostic origins for the Testament of Adam, and seems to be
relying on the earlier evaluation of Renan. Bezold was only
vaguely aware of a Greek text of the Horarium which had been
published by M. R. James.[25] Nevertheless, Bezold accepted the
Greek, sight unseen, as the source of the original Testament of
Adam.[26]

Since all the Greek texts were not edited by F. Nau until
the following year, Bezold, while waiting for the publication
of the Greek, offered a tentative evaluation of the Arabic and
Ethiopic versions which he edited. He maintained first, that
the Ethiopic was totally dependent on the Arabic; second, that
there were two recensions of the Arabic, the shorter Ar^1 and
the longer Ar^2; third, that the Syriac was not the immediate
source of Ar^1; and fourth, that the Greek was not the immediate
product of either the Arabic or Ethiopic versions.

In 1907 M. Kmosko published a major treatment of the
Testament of Adam with an introduction, Syriac text and Latin
translation.[27] Kmosko employed six Syriac manuscripts in
establishing a critical text. This was a considerable improve-
ment over Renan's text, which had employed only two Syriac
manuscripts.[28] Kmosko's work has remained the standard text
for the Testament of Adam. Kmosko identified three recensions
of the Testament of Adam from his six manuscripts:

Recension I: Codex BM Add. 14,624 folio 8^V and
                 Vatican Syriac 58 folio 115^V. Repre-
                 senting the oldest recension, these
                 manuscripts exhibit virtually the
                 same text.

Recension II: Vatican Syriac 164 folio 76^V and BM
                 Add. 25,815 folio 57^V.

Recension III: Vatican Syriac 159 folio 113^V, and
                 Arund Or 53 folio 88. The most recent
                 recension. To this recension should
                 now be added BM Add. 14,577 folio 85
                 and John Rylands Syriac manuscript 44
                 folio 27.

Kmosko began with the assumption that the Testament of
Adam was the work of Christian heretics, though he, like Hort,
rejected Renan's claim that it was a product of Gnosticism.
Kmosko further whittled down the limits of the actual testament
by suggesting that the second section, the Prophecy, had originally been part of the "cycle called the Cave of Treasures."
For Kmosko, the Testament of Adam proper was the first section
alone--the Horarium. He further suggested that the hours of the
day were an inferior addition to the original text which had
contained only the hours of the night.

While Kmosko was willing to admit that the author of the
Horarium may have possessed some talent, he shared the negative
bias of Renan and others toward this document and felt that on
the whole the Testament of Adam "smells mostly of superstition"
and was far from orthodoxy.[29] Kmosko was the first scholar to
reject completely the Jewish origin of the Testament of Adam
and was the first to attribute it in its entirety to late Christian heterodoxy.

In the same volume which contains Kmosko's article, indeed
directly following that article, F. Nau wrote[30] concerning the
Paris magical transcript 2419 which had first been cited by
M. R. James, and which contained the Horarium from the Testament
of Adam. Nau had found three other Greek manuscripts similar
to MS 2419 which also contained the Horarium. One of these was
attributed to Apollonius of Tyana, thus settling the question
of which Apollonius was meant in the attribution of Paris 2419.
As Kmosko had denied the Jewish character of the Testament of
Adam, Nau now denied its Christianity. He contended that the
Horarium, at least, was actually a product of the pagan magician Apollonius of Tyana, and that it had only been much later
incorporated into the Jewish and Christian traditions about
Adam. His conclusions have been almost universally rejected
for reasons which will be discussed below.[31]

In 1922, A. Götze published a lengthy treatment of the Cave
of Treasures. He dismissed the argument for dating the document
around the sixth century and argued that the sources of the Cave
of Treasures reached back to the third and perhaps even to the
second century A.D.[32] Götze, like Renan and Hort, maintained
originally that all of the Adam material could be traced back

to a single pre-Christian "Book of Adam." He did not directly
address the problem of the relationship between the Cave of
Treasures and the Testament of Adam, but did indicate that the
Testament must be treated as a separate document which had been
incorporated into the Cave of Treasures in an early period.[33]

Götze postulated two stages in the formation of the extant
Cave of Treasures. He suggested that there was first an
Urschatzhöhle, formed from very old traditions, which circulated before the fourth century A.D. The Testament of Adam, he
maintained, must already have stood in this early form of the
Cave of Treasures. Later, a Nestorian redactor substantially
reworked the Schatzhöhle into its present form in about the
seventh century A.D. This redactor omitted the Testament of
Adam, according to Götze, but left behind traces of the excised
work by which we can know that it once formed a part of the
original.[34] Götze felt that the Arabic, and therefore the
Ethiopic which is dependent upon the Arabic, is a translation
of the *Urschatzhöhle* before its revision by the Nestorian
redactor and thus preserves the original order of the composition including the Testament of Adam. This would explain why
the testament is not found in the extant Syriac manuscripts of
the Cave of Treasures, although these same manuscripts contain
material compatible with the testament, for example, the repetition of the scene where Adam calls his posterity together
at his death bed.

Two years after the publication of his major article on
the Cave of Treasures, Götze published another in which he
modified his views on the relationship between the Testament of
Adam and the Cave of Treasures.[35] First, Götze made explicit
his previous implication that the testament was a Gnostic work.
Second, he modified his previous insistence that the Testament
of Adam must once have stood in the *Urschatzhöhle*. Götze was
now attracted to the hypothesis that the testament was added to
the Arabic version rather than omitted from the latter Syriac
recension, and allowed that it might not have been the Testament
of Adam which dropped out of the Syriac after all, but rather
certain "revelations to Seth about the Messiah, the three pre-
cious offerings and the Magi." Therefore, Götze concluded, the
Testament of Adam originally had nothing to do with the Cave
of Treasures.[36]

These conclusions of Götze's are of particular interest in connection with the findings of Z. Avalachvili who worked with the Old Georgian version of the Cave of Treasures six years later.[37] The Old Georgian version, like the Arabic, contains the Horarium and the Prophecy from the Testament of Adam, but does not contain the Hierarchy.

Avalachvili proposed, apparently independently of Götze, that the Old Georgian version might be a translation of an earlier stage of the Syriac Cave of Treasures than that found in the present manuscripts. He believed that the Old Georgian preserved the more primitive order of the Cave of Treasures which contained the Testament of Adam. He also made it clear that the Testament of Adam must originally have been an independent document.[38] In all of this Avalachvili's position concerning the Old Georgian was analogous to the earlier position of Götze in regard to the Arabic.

Avalachvili did not offer an explanation of why the Testament of Adam would have been omitted by a later Syriac redactor or why the testament could not have been added to the Cave of Treasures in the Arabic version. The Arabic might then have been the parent not only of the Ethiopic, but of the Old Georgian as well. Moreover, in defending his proposal Avalachvili is forced to employ the principle of *longior lectio potior* in relation to the proposed recension of the Cave of Treasures. Finally, both Götze and Avalachvili referred to traces of the Testament of Adam which remained in the latter Syriac recension of the Cave of Treasures, but neither offered examples of what these traces may be or why they must have come from the Testament of Adam.[39] These considerations had forced Götze to abandon in relation to the Arabic version the very position which Avalachvili espoused relative to the Old Georgian.

Avalachvili followed Renan in attributing the Hierarchy to pseudo-Dionysius the Areopagite, and accepted Nau's evaluation of the Horarium as a work of pagan magical incantations.[40] He did not consider the possibility that any part of the Testament of Adam might be of Jewish origin.

As early as 1911, S. Grebaut had treated the Ethiopic version of the Testament of Adam.[41] In Ethiopic, as in Arabic, the testament is found incorporated into the pseudo-Clementine

work which is titled in Ethiopic Qalementos (Clement). Qalementos is comprised of seven books which are supposed to be the
mysteries taught by Christ to Peter, which Peter then passed on
to Clement who wrote them down.

Grebaut followed Dillmann in the belief that the Ethiopic
Qalementos was a translation from an Arabic original. It is
identical with the Book of the Rolls edited and translated by
M. D. Gibson. The Arabic original was written, according to
Dillmann, in Egypt between A.D. 750 and 760.[42]

Grebaut also believed that the Testament of Adam was originally a self-contained document separate from both Qalementos
and the Cave of Treasures:

> Le Qalêmentos apparaît comme une compilation de
> documents anciens, tels que les *Récognitions*, la
> *Caverne des Trésors*, le *Testament d'Adam* et peut-
> être l'*Apocalypse de Pierre*, qui auraient été
> fondus ensemble par un rédacteur anonyme.[43]

Although Grebaut believed the Testament of Adam to be both
independent of and older than Qalementos and the Cave of Treasures, he did not therefore believe it to be an early Jewish or
Christian work, but followed Nau in the belief that the Greek
fragment of the Testament of Adam in the Paris magical codices
represented a pagan Greek original of which the Syriac was an
early version.[44]

One of the most careful and complete treatments of the
Testament of Adam is that of J. B. Frey published in 1928.[45]
Frey divided the Testament of Adam into three sections rather
than into Renan's four. They are the Horarium, the Prophecy,
and the Hierarchy. He insisted on the unity of the Horarium
and Prophecy, but accepted Kmosko's position that the Hierarchy
was attributed to the Testament of Adam only through scribal
error. Frey rejected Renan's thesis of Gnostic origins for the
Testament of Adam. He was not the first to do so, but he was
the first to offer cogent reasons why the testament was abso-
lutely inimical to the basic tenets of Gnosticism.[46] Frey
gently dismissed Renan's impossible identification of the Mandaeans as the forerunners of Gnosticism and repudiated his
unsubstantiated claim that the Horarium was the model for the
canonical hours.

Frey treated the sources of the Adam literature very carefully and concluded finally against Renan, Hort, and James, that
the Penitence and the Testament of Adam could not be the same
document. He was the first to take seriously the report of
Samuel of Ani that the Penitence and the Testament were separate
works, and he noted that if it were necessary to identify the
Penitence of Adam with a document extant under some other title,
the *Vita Adae et Evae*, or the Apocalypse of Moses, would make
much better candidates than the Testament of Adam. However,
Frey continued, there was no necessity of this, since an Armenian version of a Penitence of Adam had come to light and had
been published in 1896.[47] Frey's rejection of all previous
attempts to trace the various books of Adam back to a single
archetype was a major development in the study of Adam literature. The equation of the Testament, Apocalypse, Penitence,
Life, and Book of Adam had been an *a priori* assumption of
critics for three quarters of a century, and was rendered toler-
able perhaps more than anything else by the lack of manuscript
evidence available at the time. But by 1928, when Frey's article was published, enough manuscript copies of diverse books of
Adam had come to light finally to invalidate the old equation.
Frey was the first to realize that in the Adam literature we
are dealing not with several reproductions of a single original,
but rather with a multiplicity of texts and traditions.

Frey concluded his excellent treatment of the Testament of
Adam with his reasons for placing the document in an early
Jewish, rather than a late Christian, setting. These rest pri-
marily on parallels to apocalyptic and rabbinic literature.

After the flurry of attention received in the 1920s, the
Testament of Adam was ignored except for minor bibliographical
entries for a period of almost fifty years. In the meantime,
its very existence has been forgotten, even by specialists in
the field of the Pseudepigrapha. It was not until 1972 that a
treatment of the Testament of Adam, the only article devoted to
it since 1928, was published by G. J. Reinink.[48] Reinink,
better informed than earlier critics about the nature of Gnosticism by virtue of the discoveries of the last half century,
rejects the specifically Gnostic origins postulated by most of
those critics. But Reinink does credit Renan for having focused

upon what he sees as the main problem of the testament, namely
the problem of its origin. Reinink accepts the judgment of
Kmosko that the Hierarchy should not be considered part of the
original document. However, contrary to Kmosko he believes that
the Horarium and the Prophecy form a unity. The major strength
of Reinink's treatment is found in his strict severance of the
Testament of Adam from the Cave of Treasures, reversing a trend
which had reached its fullest expression in Kmosko's treatment
of the testament. Reinink is certainly correct in throwing out
the widely accepted assumption that the Testament of Adam was
somehow dependent upon the other work. He rejects this assumption for three basic reasons. First, Reinink shows that what
he believes to be the major focus of the Cave of Treasures--the
journey of the corpse of Adam to Golgotha, the place of its
ultimate salvation--is completely absent in the testament.
Second, in the testament Adam is not buried in a sacred cavern
as in the Cave of Treasures, but in the City of Enoch which
lies in the East. Third, the burial of Adam by angels and
heavenly powers and the darkening of the sun and moon at his
death are elements foreign to the Cave of Treasures, but which
are found in the *Vita Adae et Evae*.

Reinink reviews the conclusions of Götze concerning the
relationship of the testament to the Cave of Treasures, noting
that since the testament is found in the Arabic version of the
Cave of Treasures, but not in the Syriac, there are only two
possibilities: either the Testament of Adam was added in the
translation to Arabic or else it was dropped out of the Syriac
in a later recension. Reinink offers three reasons why he
feels the testament was added to the Arabic version.[49] First,
the Arabic Testament of Adam follows the text type witnessed by
British Museum manuscript Arundel Oriental 53 (E) and by Vatican
Syriac 159 (F). This text type is secondary to that witnessed
by British Museum Additional manuscript 14,624 (A) and by
Vatican Syriac 58 (B), and contains many expansions over the
readings in A and B. In addition, the Arabic version expands
even the longer readings of E and F. Second, the Testament of
Adam is foreign to its context in the Arabic version. It is
appended to the words of Adam *after* the formulae which are used
throughout the Cave of Treasures to terminate the final words

of the Patriarchs. Third, in the Cave of Treasures the tradition which was handed down from Adam by the Patriarchs is trans-
mitted orally, while in the testament it is explicitly stated
that the tradition was written down by Seth and kept in the
cavern with the other holy objects. For these reasons Reinink
maintains that the Cave of Treasures cannot be used as an immediate source for the reconstruction and delimitation of the
Testament of Adam.[50]

In addition, Reinink, like James, does not feel that the
Greek texts found in the Paris, Berlin and Bonn manuscripts
should be used as primary sources for the Testament of Adam.
In support of this he points out that the Greek is dependent
upon the text type represented by Syriac E and F and preserves
many of its errors. Further, he asserts that the emphasis of
the Horarium in the Syriac and Arabic is cosmological while the
emphasis of the Greek from the Paris manuscripts is on the
magical significance of the hours.

Reinink is the only scholar so far to discuss the Testament
of Adam in connection with the Gnostic Apocalypse of Adam from
Nag Hammadi. He concludes that there are several parallels
between the two documents which are too close to be accidental.
And although he had rejected a specific Gnostic origin for the
Testament of Adam, he concludes that the parallels with the
Apocalypse point to an origin within an "Adamo-Sethianischen"
cycle of literature that reaches back to ancient Jewish traditions. However, Reinink maintains that in its present form the
Testament of Adam is a Christian work. He does not feel that
the exact origin of the Testament of Adam can be ascertained at
present, although the role of the Cave of Treasures[51] and of
the Magi in the text indicates to him a Syrian-Persian proven-
ance.

Another recent treatment of the Testament of Adam is found
in the summary of Adam literature by A. M. Denis.[52] Denis
treats the Adam literature generally, and the Testament of Adam
in particular, as a cycle of traditions and documents of which
the Testament of Adam was only a part. These compositions,
while related thematically, are not necessarily derived from
one another. This approach to the Adam literature, in continu-
ity with that of J. B. Frey, allows Denis to treat the spectrum

of Adam literature in all its diversity without forcing the
individual books into artifical relationships to each other.

Denis uses the tripartite division of the Testament of
Adam suggested by Frey and agrees with him that only the first
two sections, the Horarium and the Prophecy, are from the original Testament of Adam, and that the third section or Hierarchy
was attributed incorrectly to Adam by the Syriac scribe. Denis
also carefully disassociates the Testament of Adam from the Cave
of Treasures and postulates that the testament is a relic from
a primitive Life of Adam. In relating the various documents of
the Adam cycle to one another Denis offers several possible
textual or literary geneologies to explain the evolution of the
tradition but declines to attempt a solution. Although Denis
begins by properly treating the Adam literature as a cycle of
tradition, this last portion of his article represents a step
backwards as it is an attempt once again to trace all the books
of Adam back to a single document.

A brief note on the Testament of Adam is found in James H.
Charlesworth's *Pseudepigrapha and Modern Research*, where it is
discussed in connection with the Cave of Treasures. Charlesworth posits a Jewish origin for the testament and argues correctly for its inclusion within the Pseudepigrapha. He further
suggests that the testament is independent of and prior to the
Cave of Treasures, that the Prophecy may date from the late
second century A.D., and that the Horarium, because it is con-
spicuously free of Christian elements, may be even earlier.[53]

The Changing Critical Perspective

The major factors which now call for a fresh treatment of
the Testament of Adam and which are also primarily responsible
for the current renaissance in the study of the Pseudepigrapha
are (1) the proliferation of manuscript evidence and (2) the
changing critical view as to the nature of Judaism, Christianity, and Gnosticism and of their relationships to each other.
The following brief treatment is intended only to document the
shift in scholarly thinking generally and is not intended to be
a thorough treatment of the positions involved.

Palestinian vs. Hellenistic Judaism:
From Moore to Davies

The critical view of the nature of first century Judaism
has changed markedly since the early decades of this century.
At that time scholars tended to see Judaism as a monolithic edifice, very much like the rabbinic picture presented in Talmudic
times, an edifice which G. F. Moore called "a normative type of
Judaism."[54] Apocalyptic and sectarian Judaism, of which little
enough was known before the later manuscript discoveries, were
viewed by Moore and others as strictly peripheral movements on
the fringes of Judaism. Moore insisted that in the intertestamental period Judaism was dominated by the Pharisaic element of
Jewish piety and that any historical treatment of Judaism in
this period should address itself to the Pharisaic-rabbinic
"norm" *to the exclusion* of other elements as primary sources.
When Moore did use the so-called Pseudepigrapha, he insisted on
interpreting it through the rabbinic norm.

> . . . inasmuch as these writings have *never* been
> *recognized* by Judaism, it is a fallacy of method
> for the historian to make them a primary source
> for the eschatology of Judaism, much more to *con-
> taminate* its theology with them.[55] [Italics mine]

In short, Moore imposed upon intertestamental Judaism a model
which could be proven only for Mishnaic or, at earliest, post-
Jamnian Judaism.[56]

Since the normative view could not accommodate apocalyptic
Judaism, the apocalyptic tradition and apocalyptic literature
were treated as aberrations and were not allowed to inform any
discussions on the nature of Judaism. This antagonism towards
apocalyptic spilled over into the study of the New Testament
where there was a tendency among some scholars to try and
exclude apocalyptic from its place in the tradition.[57] This
antagonism toward apocalyptic is still a hidden agenda behind
much of the present discussion of biblical and intertestamental
literature.[58]

A corollary to Moore's view was that "normative Judaism"
was seen in contradistinction to a hellenistic Judaism. In the
minds of scholars two distinct categories emerged, the Judaism
of Palestine and the Judaism of the Diaspora. Palestinian Judaism was characterized as more insular, more thoroughly Semitic

and more conservatively traditional, while Diaspora Judaism was
seen as more cosmopolitan, more hellenistic, and more syncre-
tistic. The Judaism of Philo was contrasted with that of
Hillel, and in the inevitable transference and application of
the corollary to Christianity, Paul was contrasted with Peter.
Although the principals could be rearranged (e.g. A. Schweitzer
preferred to cast Paul as a Palestinian against John as a
hellenist), it is evident that the categories of hellenistic vs.
Palestinian Judaism were the same.[59]

By 1950, however, the old paradigm had become suspect in
many circles for several reasons. The works of G. Scholem
demonstrated that apocalyptic and mystical expression were not
aberrations within the mainstream, but were in fact elements
native to the very heart of Judaism.[60] The work of E. R. Goodenough and others established that Palestine had in fact readily
adopted hellenistic forms in art, architecture, and even in
religious symbolism.[61] The disqualification by Moore and others
of a large segment of the intertestamental literature became
particularly suspect:

> Phenomenologically, "normative" Talmudic Judaism
> cannot be said to have existed at all, . . . There
> is considerable reason to suppose, however, that
> local variations and modulations of ideas, emphasis,
> and interpretation of law and doctrine were far
> more substantial than we have hitherto supposed.
> In attempting to understand the varied phenomena of
> Judaism in this period, therefore, we must regard
> all sources of information as equally relevant, and,
> in such a context, equally "normative."[62]

Some of the earliest and most consistent forces towards the
increasing abandonment of the old view were the works of D.
Daube, M. Smith, and W. D. Davies. Davies consistently empha-
sized *both* aspects of the new perspective: the "Palestinian"
Jewishness of the Diaspora, *and* the penetrating hellenism of
Palestine. In his book, *Paul and Rabbinic Judaism*, Davies
chose to interpret Pauline theology primarily by means of Jewish
paradigms, while not wholly ruling out hellenistic ones. Davies
saw that Paul could legitimately be a hellenistic Jew without
being outside the mainstream of Judaism, that intertestamental
Judaism was not confined to a rabbinic norm, and that it was
incorrect to divide it into sharply contrasting Palestinian and
hellenistic categories.[63]

E. P. Sanders has recently evaluated the significance of
Davies' work in respect to its impact on the old monolithic
view:

> It is not that Davies was the first to observe Hell-
> enistic influences in Palestinian Judaism or Jewish
> influences in Hellenism--in his comments on these
> points he always refers to the work of others--or
> that he himself spent his research time in investi-
> gating and exploring the interpenetration. Rather
> he helped call the interpenetration to the attention
> of New Testament scholars and showed that ignoring
> it had led to an oversimplified view of New Testament
> backgrounds. Professor Davies' voice has been one
> of the principal factors in making the current gen-
> eration of New Testament scholars aware of the com-
> plexities of the question of the conceptual thought-
> worlds in which the New Testament literature was
> written.[64]

However, all of this notwithstanding, the greatest single
factor in the changing view of the nature of Judaism was
undoubtedly the discovery and analysis of the Dead Sea Scrolls
and other literature of the intertestamental period. The impact
of the Scrolls was great enough to move W. F. Albright in 1952
to call for a rewriting of all works dealing with the background
of the New Testament.[65] The Dead Sea Scrolls made it readily
apparent that many of the elements which had formerly been
attributed to hellenistic Judaism were in fact indigenous among
Palestinian Jews. Further, the scrolls revealed that intertestamental Judaism was not the homogenous structure that Moore
had believed. In the words of Millar Burrows:

> The doctrines and practices of the covenanters
> substantially enrich our knowledge of Judaism at the
> time just before and during the origin and early
> growth of Christianity. It is now abundantly clear
> that we cannot understand the Judaism of the Roman
> period simply in terms of the Pharisees and Saddu-
> cees [the "normative" Judaism of Moore]. The tree
> whose trunk was the Old Testament had then many
> branches which later were lopped off or withered
> away.
>
> The enlarged understanding of Judaism contributes
> in turn to our understanding of the New Testament, in
> its relation to its background and derivation, and
> all the more so because the beliefs, ideals, organi-
> zation, and rites of the covenanters, as compared
> with those of the early church, exhibit both
> impressive similarities and even more significant
> contrasts.[66]

The weight of the literary evidence presented by the
scrolls added to that of the archeological evidence and to previous arguments by careful scholars proved overwhelming to the
monolithic view. To quote Davies: "It is not necessary to
labor the obvious. The old dichotomy between Palestinian and
Diaspora Hellenistic Judaism is no longer tenable."[67]

Judaism and Christianity:
From Moore to Slingerland

A further tendency of the monolithic view had been the
sharp contradistinction of Judaism and Christianity in the first
century A.D. It was only reasonable that if "normative" Judaism
was characterized as a non-apocalyptic, non-eschatological and
non-mystical stream of Pharisaic Torah piety, that Christianity
should be seen as a movement totally separate and distinct from
it. Nevertheless, it was inevitable once the bars between
hellenistic and Palestinian Judaism were pulled down and it
had been generally accepted that Judaism was a more heterogenous
phenomenon than Moore allowed, that one of the first repercus-
sions would be a reappraisal of the relationship between
Christians and Jews in the first century. When the picture of
Judaism had been corrected to include more heterodox elements,
much of what had formerly been thought original to Christianity
was seen to have obvious Jewish roots.[68]

Recent scholarship has tended to reject the stark opposi-
tion of church and synagogue in the early first century.
Rather, earliest Christianity is now seen to have been a sect
within Judaism, and the early Christian a heterodox Jew. Typical of this view is the following by L. Martyn:

> All the way from the arrest of Peter and John in
> chapter 3 to Paul's appearance (now as a Christian)
> before the Sanhedrin in chapter 23, Acts paints a
> picture in which Jewish authorities view the church
> as essentially subject to Jewish law. That is to
> say, the church is viewed by the Jewish authorities
> as a sect, a bothersome one to be sure, but still
> a sect which remained within the bosom of Judaism.[69]

D. R. A. Hare has shown that the methods employed by Jews in
the harrassment of Christians before A.D. 70 reflect an attempt
at internal discipline rather than an attack on a non-Jewish
religion.[70]

The final split between Judaism and Christianity is now
generally dated toward the end of the first century, and is
seen to have been a result of several factors. First, the refu-
sal of Christians to participate in the Jewish revolt of A.D.
70 separated them from the nationalistic aspirations of Israel.
Second, the consolidation of Judaism in the Pharisaic mold after
A.D. 70 and the subsequent introduction, around A.D. 85, of the
Birkath ha-Minim made it increasingly impossible for Christians
to remain in the synagogues.[71]

> No evidence of organized opposition to the
> Christian movement is found prior to the destruc-
> tion of the Temple. The insertion of the Birkath
> ha-Minim indicates that rabbinic authorities found
> it necessary to oppose minority sects in an attempt
> to consolidate their position. There is no evidence,
> however, of any attempt on their part to initiate
> an organized campaign of violence against Christians.[72]

Third, the influx of uncircumcised Gentiles into the Christian
church, the fruit of the Gentile mission, made the close association of Christians and Torah-observing Jews impossible.

Contemporary scholars, having learned from the demise of
Moore's thesis, are more aware of "the complexity of the Christian movement itself which included a significant number of
loyal Pharisees."[73] As Wayne Meeks has recently put it, "Christianity was never a monolithic society, but a polymorphous
movement, the vector constituted by tensions in many direc-
tions."[74]

But once again, the greatest factor in the widening perspective upon earliest Christianity has been the discovery of
additional manuscript evidence. The Dead Sea Scrolls in particular have revealed the presence of much in sectarian Judaism
which may have influenced the beliefs and practices of the
early church. The impact of the Scrolls in bringing the investigation of Christian origins back to Palestinian, or at least
to Jewish, soil must not be held lightly.[75] Once again, the
weight of the Scrolls has been an important factor in the shifting of the scales.

The current trend of minimizing the distinctions between
Christianity and Judaism before A.D. 70 has recently led H. D.
Slingerland to propose a bold hypothesis which carries the new
approach to its logical extreme. Slingerland suggests that the

distinction between Jewish and Christian be thrown out entirely
in reqard to pre-70 literature whose authorship is in question
and that the texts be allowed as sources for the study of *both*
Judaism and Christianity.[76] It is Slingerland's contention
that since Christianity before A.D. 70 was in its own self-
consciousness a Jewish sect, those elements in pre-70 Christian
literature which cannot be shown to be Christian in an exclusive
sense should be allowed to inform our understanding of the
Judaism of the period as well. Slingerland places the burden
of proof on those who would disallow the use of such passages
except where they can be shown by other criteria to be exclusively Christian. Slingerland concludes that relative to the
period before A.D. 70 the debate over the Jewish or Christian
authorship of intertestamental writings may be meaningless and
that to a large extent the terms Jewish and Christian, in this
period, represent a distinction without a difference.

It is not the purpose of the present study to evaluate the
relative merit of Slingerland's position, but rather to illus-
trate by citing it how the critical pendulum has swung from one
extreme to the other; from earlier critics who posited a "normative" Judaism clearly distinct from Christianity, to those who
now would propose a radical elimination of distinctions between
the two. Correctly or incorrectly, for good reasons and bad,
the critical view of the nature of Judaism and Christianity has
changed to a great extent since the major discussions of the
Testament of Adam took place at the beginning of this century.
This change calls for a reexamination and reevaluation, not
only of the Testament of Adam, but of all the intertestamental
literature in terms of the positive insights of the new views.

The Reappraisal of Gnosticism:
From Reitzenstein to MacRae

There were generally two different but related views on
the origins of Gnosticism in early critical scholarship. The
first view was that Gnosticism was a phenomenon wholly foreign
and external to Christianity and Judaism (again, as informed by
the old monolithic categories), inimical to those religions,
and against which they struggled mightily and, for the most
part, successfully. The second view held that Gnosticism was a
bastard child of Christianity and/or Judaism, morally and

intellectually impoverished, spawned in the minds of the foolish
and ignorant by the contaminating influences of the external
forces of hellenism.

The former view was proposed mainly by the followers of
R. Reitzenstein and the *religionsgeschichtliche Schule* who saw
Gnosticism as the product of Iranian religion imposed upon the
hellenistic and Judeo-Christian West.[77] This position conformed
well to the monolithic view of Judaism, since it attributed the
Gnostic phenomenon to entirely external sources. And although
the exact point of origin may have been debated, few scholars
doubted the canon that Gnosticism could *not* have originated
within the Judeo-Christian tradition. As long as the old definition of a "normative Judaism" held sway, the possibility of
discovering any Jewish roots for Gnosticism was unlikely to
occur, since it was ruled out of court by definition.

The second of the earlier views mentioned above was due in
part to the evaluation of Gnosticism by "orthodox" writers both
ancient and modern. We have already noted the very caustic
attitude of Assemani, Renan, and others toward Gnosticism.
However, as scholars have been more and more able to dissociate
themselves from the use of such categories as "orthodoxy" and
"heresy" a much more objective picture of the nature of Gnosticism has become possible.[78] The discovery of a large group
of Gnostic texts at Nag Hammadi has established both the aesthe-
tic beauty and intellectual complexity of many Gnostic works.

The main thrust of Reitzenstein's theory, that Gnosticism
was an external force working on Judaism and Christianity, has
been seriously questioned for several reasons. First, Reitzenstein's original theory was based upon supposed parallels
between Zoroastrian and Gnostic concepts and rituals. As it
later turned out, many of these parallels were drawn from texts
which were not Iranian but Manichaean and demonstrably later
than their Gnostic parallels.[79] Second, scholars have come to
realize the methodological fallacy of any theory of origins
based primarily on the use of literary "parallels." Third, a
reexamination of much of the Iranian material indicates that it
is not as "parallel" as Reitzenstein, who was not an Iranologist,
had thought.[80] Fourth, and most important, it has become increasingly evident that the vocabulary and imagery of Gnosticism

is to a large extent that of the biblical tradition. Granted,
these are often employed in a novel manner, but the basic materials out of which Gnosticism is built are generally biblical.
As G. MacRae correctly emphasizes, "the familiarity which Gnostic sources show toward details of Jewish thought is hardly one
that we could expect non-Jews to have."[81]

For these reasons and others the majority of scholars,
though by no means all of them, have begun to look *within* the
biblical tradition for some of the roots of Gnosticism. MacRae
is representative of a large group of scholars who place the
origin of Gnosticism within Judaism, a move which would have
been unlikely before the collapse of the old monolithic view.
Herein lies the crux of the shift in scholarly perspective:
while Reitzenstein and the *religionsgeschichtliche Schule* saw
Gnosticism as foreign and inimical to Judaism and Christianity,
MacRae and others see it as a revolt within the circle of Judaism.

> The answer to the question must lie in the reali-
> zation that the essence of the Gnostic attitude, as
> has often been stated, is one of revolt, and it is a
> revolt against Judaism itself. Yet somehow it must
> be conceived as a revolt *within* Judaism. The poi-
> gnancy of the expression of it indicates this: the
> Wisdom of Yahweh has been a deception.[82]

Along the same lines, R. M. Grant has suggested that Gnosticism is a product of the frustrated Jewish apocalyptic hope;[83]
and O. Wintermute has shown that in the case of the Nag Hammadi
tractate On the Origin of the World (CG II, 5) the Gnostic
method of exegesis, far from being hostile to the Old Testament,
"led to a respect for the text and an assiduous attempt to interpret it skillfully in order to demonstrate wisdom which it contained."[84] Wintermute shows that the Gnostic "regard for the
authority of the Old Testament appears to be as vigorous as that
of their orthodox opponents,"[85] and that the exegesis, "took
place within circles where a proof-text from the prophet would
still represent reasonably persuasive argument."[86]

It should also be noted that the manuscripts discovered at
Nag Hammadi have largely failed to substantiate the Iranian element in Gnosticism and even those who, like H. Jonas, deny the
Jewish origins of Gnosticism must admit with Jonas that Gnosticism did at least originate "in close vicinity" to Judaism.[87]

Finally, as we have already intimated, the discovery of the
Nag Hammadi library and other Gnostic texts have had an impact
on the study of Gnosticism analogous to that of the Dead Sea
Scrolls on the study of Judaism. Documents from Nag Hammadi
such as the Apocalypse of Adam (CG V, 5) and the Apocalypse of
Zostrianos (CG VIII, 1), which undeniably reflect the biblical
tradition, have done much to strengthen the theory of the Jewish
origins of Gnosticism.[88] The discovery of such a large body of
Gnostic literature has done much to ameliorate the particularly
persistent though uncritical attitude that Gnosticism was an
"illegitimate" form of Christianity. In the days of the early
view Gnosticism, being largely an unknown quantity, had been
the trash heap for anything that would not fit into the other
categories of the monolithic view. Now the Nag Hammadi find
offers a warning against the fallacy of positing a "normative"
Gnosticism; for the Gospel of Thomas or the Acts of Peter and
the Twelve Apostles are certainly appreciably different from
such documents as the Thunderer or the Allogenes.

The two main points established from the foregoing are
these: first, that the consensus of scholarly opinion is
shifting. Gnosticism is more and more being seen as an internal
rather than external phenomenon relative to the biblical tradition. M. Mansoor correctly reports that "one of the most striking features of recent gnostic studies is the tendency to see
in Judaism the source, or at least, the main channel, through
which *Gnosis* entered the Graeco-Roman world."[89] Second, that
in its Christian manifestations Gnosticism is being thought of
less and less as an illegitimate aberration of Christianity,
smelling of superstition and quackery, and is being accepted
more and more as one of many varied forms of early Christianity.
These observations are pertinent to our study of the Testament
of Adam in view of the persistent claim that the testament was
a product of late gnostic superstition and therefore relatively
unworthy of critical attention. The attribution of the testament to the Gnostics runs like a thread throughout the history
of its critical treatment. The recent developments in the study
of Gnosticism demand a reevaluation if not a complete unravel-
ling of that thread.

The Proliferation of Manuscript Evidence

The greatest single factor in the expanded understanding of
Judaism, Christianity, and Gnosticism has been the proliferation
of manuscript evidence. From the discovery of the Dead Sea
Scrolls, the Nag Hammadi Library, and other documentary evidence
from the intertestamental period, it has become clear that the
old monolithic view and its corollaries prevalent in the first
half of this century rested to a great extent on the paucity of
information available at that time. The proliferation of manuscripts and of archaeological evidence for the period now indicates that intertestamental Judaism was a very much more vari-
egated phenomenon than had previously been believed. When
R. H. Charles, a major proponent of the monolithic view, edited
the Pseudepigrapha of the Old Testament in a work which was
to influence scholars for at least three-quarters of a century,[90]
his volume contained only 17 entries, and two of these are now
categorized with the Dead Sea Scrolls and rabbinic literature.
In his forthcoming edition of the Pseudepigrapha of the Old
Testament, J. H. Charlesworth has collected over fifty documents.
Thus our manuscript evidence for the Pseudepigrapha alone has
increased three-fold since the days of Charles. With the
increase of manuscript evidence has come a widening of our
understanding of the groups which produced the manuscripts. The
process of breaking down categories and widening the possible
extension of the term "Judaism" continues today, as witnessed
by the recent willingness on the part of scholars to accept
astrological and even magical material under the term "Judaism."[91]

The pertinence of this discussion for the study of the
Testament of Adam is witnessed by the fact that, with one exception, the critical treatment of the testament took place before
the discovery of the Dead Sea Scrolls, of the Nag Hammadi Library, and of the majority of documents to be contained in
Charlesworth's edition of the Pseudepigrapha. It is in terms
of the proliferation of manuscript evidence and of the consequently expanded understanding of what may legitimately be
labelled Jewish that, taking Albright's challenge seriously,
the Testament of Adam must be reexamined.[92] The present study
will attempt to take into account the expanded number of manuscripts, both of the Testament of Adam in particular and of the

intertestamental literature in general, and will in Chapter V attempt to place the Testament of Adam in its setting *vis-a-vis* Gnosticism, Judaism, and Christianity.

THE SYRIAC TESTAMENT OF ADAM

The Syriac Testament of Adam is found in three recensions. Recension 1 consists of two manuscripts, and contains the Horarium, with the hours of the night appearing first, and the Prophecy of Adam to Seth. Recension 2, also consists of two manuscripts and contains the Horarium and Prophecy, but adds a long section on the orders of angels which has been called the Hierarchy. The Horarium in recension 2 contains only the hours of the night. Recension 3 consists of four manuscripts and contains only the hours of the day and night, the hours of the day appearing first. One manuscript of recension 3, Vatican Syriac 159, also contains the Prophecy of Adam to Seth, but this may be due to the later influence of recensions 1 and 2.[1]

The Syriac text was first published in 1853 by E. Renan in an edition based primarily on Vatican Syriac manuscript 164 with support from Vatican Syriac 58 (manuscripts C and B, respectively), and was accompanied by a French translation with notes.[2] Renan's translation, slightly altered, was reproduced in 1856 by J. P. Migne in the *Dictionnaire des Apocryphes*.[3] In 1865, W. Wright published a portion of the Syriac text from British Museum Additional manuscript 14,624 (manuscript A) without an English translation.[4] An eclectic Syriac text employing six manuscripts was finally produced by M. Kmosko in 1907, accompanied by a Latin translation.[5] This was the only edition of the Testament of Adam to use more than two Syriac manuscripts and has since served as the standard work on the Testament of Adam. A German translation of Vatican Syriac manuscript 164 (manuscript C) was published in 1927 by P. Riessler.[6]

The eight Syriac manuscripts of the Testament of Adam date from the ninth to the eighteenth century. Two of these, British Museum Additional manuscript 14,577 (manuscript H) and John Rylands Syriac manuscript 44 (manuscript G), were not used by Kmosko in his 1907 edition of the text.[7] In every Syriac

45

manuscript the Testament of Adam appears as an independent,
self-contained work, and is clearly entitled "The Testament of
Adam." The eight Syriac manuscripts are:

A - British Museum Additional manuscript 14,624, a
    vellum codex, is the oldest of the manuscripts,
    dating from the early ninth century A.D.[8] It
    contains fifty-six vellum leaves measuring approx-
    imately 9-1/2 x 6-5/8 inches.[9] The script is
    Estrangela, written in a very good hand, on two
    columns to the page, each column containing
    between twenty-five and thirty-four lines. The
    Testament of Adam occupies folios 8[b]-10[a] and
    comes between the Testament of Ephraim and three
    discourses by Jacob of Batnae. Much of the
    manuscript is stained and torn, including folio
    8, with which the Testament of Adam begins.
    This manuscript, which serves as the base text
    for recension 1 in the edition below, contains
    both the Horarium and the Prophecy and is the
    single most important witness to the text of
    the Testament of Adam since it is both the
    oldest and exhibits the fewest expansions.

B - Vatican Syriac manuscript 58 is a paper codex
    dated A.D. 1584-6. There are two hundred and
    three folios written in Serta script with fre-
    quent rubrication. The text is written in a
    single column with seventeen lines per page.
    The Testament of Adam occupies folios 115[a]-116[b],
    and comes between the Blessing on Things Pol-
    luted and The Names and Homelands of the
    Prophets. The manuscript is stained on almost
    every page, although it is usually readable.
    The text is that of recension 1.[10]

C - Vatican Syriac manuscript 164 is a paper codex
    dated A.D. 1702, containing one hundred and
    eighty folios. The text is written in Nestor-
    ian script, in a single column, with eighteen
    lines per page. The Testament of Adam appears

on folios 75^b-77^a. Like British Museum Additional manuscript 25,875 (manuscript D),
Vatican Syriac 164 was copied in or near
Mosul, and the contents of both manuscripts
are reproduced in exactly the same order.[11]
Since manuscript D is dated A.D. 1709, seven
years later than C, it is possible that C is
the exemplar of or perhaps a brother to D.
The manuscript contains the Horarium and the
Prophecy, and is also the sole witness for a
third section on the orders of angels, which
may have been attributed to Adam by scribal
error. This manuscript serves below as the
base text for recension 2.[12]

D - British Museum Additional manuscript 25,865
    is a paper codex dated in the year A.D. 1709-10.
    It measures approximately 8-7/8 x 6-1/8 inches
    and is written in a good Nestorian hand. It
    is a long manuscript, containing three hundred
    and sixty-two folios. The text is written
    two columns to the page, each column containing
    twenty-eight lines. The Testament of Adam,
    which begins and ends with rubrics, is found
    on folios 57^b-58^b, between The Questions of
    Ezra the Scribe and The Revelation and Visions
    of the Just of Old and of the True Prophets
    Regarding the Dispensation of the Messiah.
    The manuscript is well preserved but contains
    only the Prophecy of Adam to Seth and is the
    only one of the eight manuscripts to omit the
    Horarium. This manuscript is either a copy of
    or comes from the same exemplar as manuscript
    C, since both were copied in the same area and
    the readings of each are identical (allowing
    for errors of the copyist), although D, which is
    seven years younger than C, contains only the
    Prophecy. Both manuscripts also contain the
    Syriac Cave of Treasures, which has often erro-
    neously been considered the source of the
    Testament of Adam.[13]

E - Arundel Oriental manuscript 53, at the British
Library, is a paper codex dated A.D. 1536. It
contains ninety-five folios written in a single
column in Serta script, with between twenty-
eight and thirty-two lines per page. The Testament of Adam is found on folios 88[b]-88[a].
The numeration of the folios is backward because
the manuscript was numbered upside down, and
from back to front. Some of its compositions
are in Karshuni, some in Syriac. This manuscript
contains only the Horarium, and belongs to recension 3.[14]

F - Vatican Syriac manuscript 159 is a paper codex
written between A.D. 1628 and 1632. It is an
extremely long manuscript, containing four
hundred and sixty-seven folios written two
columns to the page in an extremely small and
crowded Serta script with frequent rubrication.[15]
There are between fifty and fifty-five lines
per column though the scribe sometimes leaves
portions of a column blank. Although M. Kmosko
and A. Baumstark indicate that the Testament
of Adam is found on folios 113[b]-114[a], this is
no longer correct.[16] The Testament of Adam is
currently located within this manuscript on
folios 246[b]-247[a].[17] This is the only manuscript
of recension 3 to contain the Prophecy of Adam
to Seth, and for this reason it is used as the
base text for recension 3 below.[18]

G - John Rylands Syriac manuscript 44 is a paper
codex of the fifteenth century, containing
one hundred and thirty-four lines per page.
It is written in extremely bad Nestorian
script, A. Mingana calling it "The most unsatisfactory Syriac MS. which I have ever seen."[19]
The Testament of Adam is found on folio 27,
and is set off by rubrics and two crosses in
the margin. The text belongs to recension 3
and was not used by Kmosko in his edition of

1907. This manuscript also contains the
only known copy of the Treatise of Shem and
much other astrological material.[20]

H - British Museum Additional manuscript 14,577
is a vellum codex of the late ninth century,
and is the earliest witness of recension 3.
It contains one hundred and thirty folios
and measures approximately 10-3/8 x 7-3/8
inches. There are two columns to the page,
each column containing between thirty-two and
thirty-six lines. The text is written in
good Estrangela which is only slightly less
handsome than that of manuscript A. This manuscript contains only the Horarium which is
found on folio 85, coming between the Questions
of Isaac and an anonymous and untitled dialogue
between a master and his disciple. This manuscript was not used by Kmosko in his 1907
edition of the Syriac text.[21]

Although the Syriac Testament of Adam has been translated
into Latin, French and German, it has never before been translated into English.[22] In the text and translation offered
below, it seemed preferable to use an actual text to represent
each of the three recensions rather than construct an eclectic,
and therefore hypothetical, text.[23] Manuscript A has been
chosen to represent recension 1 since it is the older of two
witnesses which seldom disagree. Manuscript C has been chosen
to represent recension 2 because it is the only Syriac manuscript which contains the section on the orders of angels and
because the alternative, manuscript D, is clearly defective.
Manuscript F has been chosen to represent recension 3 because
it contains both the Horarium and the Prophecy.

In the English translation below, parentheses indicate
words added to make good English sense. Brackets represent
editorial additions beyond those required for good English, or
restorations suggested by the author based on other witnesses.
Underscoring in the English translation indicates rubrication
in the Syriac manuscript. In several of the manuscripts the
scribe frequently omits the seyame, the two dots which signify

the plural. This is common in older manuscripts, and such omis-
sions will not be noted below. Footnotes to parallels in other
literature which apply to all three recensions are not repeated
in the notes to recensions 2 and 3. The text of all eight
Syriac manuscripts has been taken from photographs graciously
provided by the authorities of the British Library (manuscripts
A, D, E and H), the Vatican Library (manuscripts B, C and F),
and the John Rylands Library (manuscript G).[24] The text below
has been reproduced lithographically from the photographs. Due
to the limitations of this process, some of the reproductions
have been retouched slightly to clarify letters which are
legible in the photographs, but not in the facsimiles. However,
in no case has any restoration been attempted where a letter is
not clearly discernible in the photograph.

Syriac Manuscripts of the Testament of Adam

Recension	MS	Catalogue No.	Folios	Date
1	A:	BM Add 14,624	8^b-10^a	early 9th cent.
	B:	Vat Syr 58	115^a-116^b	late 16th cent.
2	C:	Vat Syr 164	75^b-77^a	early 18th cent.
	D:	BM Add 25,875	57^b-58^b	early 18th cent.
3	E:	Arund Or 53	88^b-88^a	16th cent.
	F:	Vat Syr 159	246^b-247^a	17th cent.
	G:	Rylands 44*	27^a-27^b	15th cent.
	H:	BM Add 14,577*	85^a-85^b	late 9th cent.

*not previously edited

ܬܫܡܫܬ ܫܥܝܐ[1] ܕܐܝܡ 1:1
ܡܐ ܘܠܠܝܐ[2] ܫܥܬܐ ܩܕܡܝܬܐ
ܕܠܠܝܐ: ܬܫܒܘܚܬܐ ܕܫܐ̈ܕܐ.
ܘܒܗܿ ܫܥܬܐ ܠܐ
ܡ̈ܙܝܩܝܢ ܠܐ ܦܓܥܝܢ[3] ܒܒܢ̈ܝ
[4] ܐܢܫܐ. ܫܥܬܐ ܕܬܪ̈ܬܝܢ 2
ܬܫܒܘܚܬܐ ܕܝ̈ܘܢܐ.
ܫܥܬܐ ܕܬܠܬ[5] ܬܫܒܘܚܬ 3
ܕܢ̈ܘܢܐ[6] ܘܕܢܘܪܐ ܘܕܟܠܗ
ܬܗ̈ܘܡܐ[7] ܬܚ̈ܬܝܐ. ܫܥܬܐ 4
ܕܐܪܒܥ ܩܕܝܫ ܕܣܪ̈ܦܐ
ܗܟܢܐ ܫܡܥ ܗܘܝܬ
ܩܕܡ ܕܐܣܟܠ. ܩܠ
ܓܦ̈ܝܗܘܢ ܒܦܪܕܝܣܐ. ܟܕ
ܢܩܫܝܢ ܕܝܢ ܣܪ̈ܦܐ ܒܩܠܐ
ܕܩܘܕܫܐ ܬܠܝܬܝܐ. ܘܡܢ
ܕܥܒܪܬ ܥܠ ܢܡܘܣܐ
ܠܐ ܫܡܥܬ ܗܘ ܩܠܐ.
ܫܥܬܐ ܕܚܡܫ ܬܫܒܘܚܬܐ 5
ܕܡ̈ܝܐ ܕܠܥܠ ܡܢ ܫܡܝܐ.
ܗܟܢܐ ܫܡܥ[8] ܗܘܝܬ ܐܢܐ
ܘܡܠܐܟ̈ܐ ܩܠܐ ܕܓ̈ܠܠܐ

---

[1] B: ܕܫܥܝܬܐ.

[2] B: adds ܘܕܠܠܝܐ.

[3] B: ܦܓܥܝܢ.

[4] B: ܕܬܪܬܝܢ.

[5] B: ܕܬܠܬ.

[6] Read with B: ܕܢܘܢܐ.

[7] B:adds ܬܗܘܡܐ (dittography).

[8] B: ܫܡܥܬ.

Recension 1
The Testament of Our Father Adam

1:1   The first hour of the night:[a] the praise of the
      demons. And in that hour (they) neither injure
      nor harm any human being.

2   The second hour: the praise of the doves.[b]

3   The third hour: the praise of the fi[s]h and of
      fire and of all the depths below.[c]

4   The fourth hour: the tri[s]hagion of the sera-
      phim.[d] Thus I used to hear, before I sinned,
      the sound of their wings in paradise when the
      seraphim were beating (them) with the sound of
      their trishagia.[e] But after I transgressed
      against the law, I did not hear that sound (any
      longer).[f]

5   The fifth hour: the praise of the waters that
      are above heaven.[g] Thus I myself used to
      hear, with the angels, the sound[h] of mighty

---

a.   Note that in recension 1, as in the Jewish reckoning,
the day begins with the hours of the night. Cf. Gen 1:5.

b.   It is likely that recension 1 preserves the original
reading here, since evening is the correct time for doves to
roost and coo. Compare the tenth hour of the night where the
roosters crow at dawn. Recensions 2 and 3 confuse ܟܝܘܢܐ (doves)
with ܢܘܢܐ (fish).

c.   Ps 148:7-8.

d.   Isa 6:1-6.

e.   The image is taken ultimately from Isa 6:2 where the
seraphim fly about while shouting their praises. See also Ezek
3:13.

f.   2 Bar 4:3.

g.   Gen 1:7-8.

h.   Or, "both the angels (and) the sound."

6

7

8

9

10

---

[1] B: ܘܗ.

[2] B: ܐܬܐ.

[3] Read with B: ܬܘܒܢ.

[4] B: ܪܕܕ.

[5] B: ܬܐܘܣܟ.

waves,[a] a sign which would inspire them to
raise a hymn of praise to the Creator.

6   The sixth hour: the construction of clouds and
     the great fear which occurs at midnight.[b]

7   The seventh hour: the viewing of their powers[c]
     when the waters are sleeping. And in that hour
     the waters are taken up and the priest of God
     mixes them with consecrated oil and anoints
     those who are afflicted and (they) rest.[d]

8   The eighth hour: the springing up of the grass
     of the earth while the dew is descending from
     heaven.[e]

9   The ninth hour: the praise of the cherubim.

10   The tenth hour: the praise of human beings,
     and opening the gate of heaven [where] the
     prayers of all living things enter and worship
     and depart. And in that hour whatever a man
     will ask from God is given to him when the
     seraphim and the roosters beat their wings.[f]

---

a. Cf. Ezek 1:24. MS E reads "wheels," an attractive
reading in view of the similar passage in 3En 19:5-6, "And
between one wheel and the other earthquake is roaring and thunder is thundering. And when the time draws near for the recital
of the *Song*, (then) the multitudes of wheels are moved, the
multitude of clouds tremble...all the troops are in fear," H.
Odeberg, *3 Enoch or The Hebrew Book of Enoch* (Cambridge: Cambridge University Press, 1928; reprint ed. New York: KTAV,
1973), p. 69. Compare with verses 5 and 6 above.

b. 2Bar 29:7.

c. MS E reads "beasts", mistaking ܚܝܘܬܐ for ܚܝܠܐ. This
error is repeated in the Greek text.

d. James 5:14-5, m. Shabbat 14.4, ApMos 9:3, *Vita* 36:2,
41:3.

e. 3Bar 10:10.

f. The behavior of roosters in beating their wings and
crowing at the rising sun is equated with the behavior of the
seraphim who beat their wings and sing praises to God. Compare
the similar passage at 3Bar 6:16, and also Ber 60b.

---

[1] B: .

[2] Read with B: .

[3] Read with B: .

[4] Read with B: .

[5] Read with B: .

[6] Read with B: .

[7] B: .

[8] B is illegible here.

11 The eleventh hour: joy in all the earth while
the sun is rising from paradise, and shining
forth upon creation.[a]

12 The twelfth hour: the awaiting of [incens]e and
the silence which is imposed [upon] all the ranks
of fire [and of win]d[b] until [all] the priests
burn incense [to] his [d]ivinity.[c] And at that
time all the powers of the heavenly (places)
are dismissed.

The End of the Hours of the Night

2:1   The Hours of the Day

The first hour of the day: the petition of the
heavenly beings.

2 The seco[nd] hour: the [p]rayer of the [a]ngels.[d]

3 The third hour: the praise of flying creatures.

4 The fourth hour: the praise of the beasts.

5 The fifth hour: the praise which is above heaven.

6 The sixth hour: the praise of the cherubim
who petition against the iniquity of our human
nature.[e]

7 The seventh hour: the entry and exit from before
God, when the prayers of all that lives enter
and worship and depart.

---

a. Note that the cooing of the doves, the crowing of the
roosters, the rising of the sun, and the burning of incense
(1:12) are all placed in the hour appropriate to each in this
recension.

b. Ps 104:4.

c. Perhaps in the temple service. The lacunae are restored
according to MS B.

d. Verses 1 and 2 are very similar to Ps 148:1-2.

e. 1En 40:6.

---

[1] B: .

[2] B: .

[3] B: .

[4] B: .

8   The eighth hour: the praise of fire and of the
    waters.

9   The ninth hour: the supplication of those angels
    who stand before the throne of majesty.

10 The tenth hour: the visitation of the waters when
    the spirit is descending and brooding over the waters
    and over the fountains.[a] And if the spirit of the
    Lo[r]d did [not] descend and brood over the waters
    and over the fountains, human beings would be injured,
    and all whom the demons saw, they would injure. And
    in that hour the waters are taken up and the priest
    of God mixes them with consecrated oil and anoints
    those who are afflicted and (they) are restored and
    (they) are healed.[b]

11 The eleventh hour: the exultation and the joy of
    the righteous.[c]

12 The twelfth hour, (the hour) of the evening: the
    [s]upplication by human beings, for the gracious
    will of God,[d] the Lord of all.

                    (The Prophecy)[e]

1   Adam said to Seth, his son: "You have heard,[f] my
    son, that God is coming into the world[g] after a long

a. Gen 1:2.

b. Cf. Verse 1:7 above p. 55, n. d.

c. The Greek reads "elect."

d. Lit. "which is with God;" compare Mt 6:10.

e. Adam's prophecy to his posterity in general, or to
Seth in particular, is also found in *Ant.* 1.2.3, ApocAd 64:2-6,
85:19-31, *Vita Adae et Evae* 25:1-2, and in the Armenian Death
of Adam (see Stone, *HTR* 59 [1966] 285).

f. The diacritical mark here indicates 2nd person; that
of B indicates 1st person: "I have heard."

g. Adam prophesies the coming of God into the world in
Vita Adae et Evae 29:2-8, and the coming of a divine "Illuminator" in ApocAd 76:8 *et passim*.

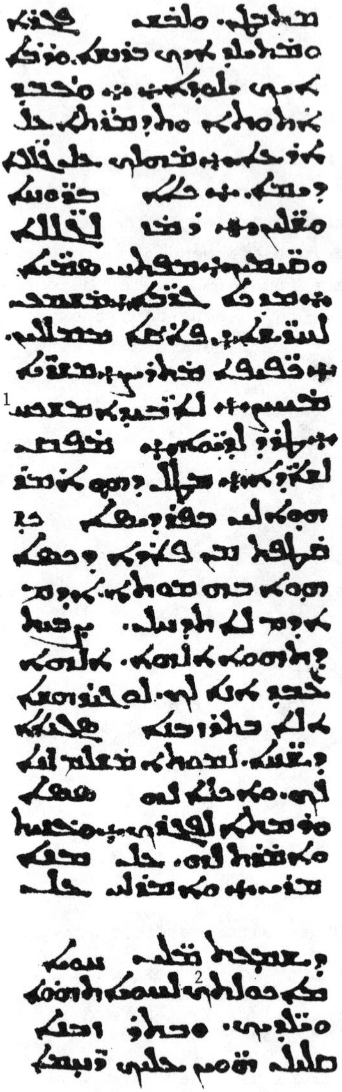

1 [illegible] 2 [illegible] 3 [illegible]

[1] B: [illegible].

[2] B: [illegible].

time,[a] conceived by a virgin and putting on a body,
both being born as a human being, and growing up as
an infant, and performing signs and wonders on the
earth, walking on the waves of the sea, rebuking
the winds and (they are) silenced, beckoning to the
waves and (they) stand still, opening (the eyes of)
the blind, cleansing the lepers, causing the deaf
to hear; the mute speak; straightening up the hunchbacked, strengthening the paralyzed, finding the lost,
driving out evil spirits, casting out demons.[b]

2   Concerning this, he spoke to me in paradise when I
picked some of the fruit in which death was hiding:
'Adam, Adam do not fear. You wanted to be a god;
a god I will make you.[c] However, not right now, but
after a period of many years.[d] I am delivering you
up to death, and the maggot and the worm[e] will
devour your body.[f]

3   And I answered and said to him: 'What for, my Lord?'
And he said to me: 'Because you listened to the
words of the serpent, you will become food[g] for the
serpent, together with your posterity. But after a
short time there will be mercy on you because you

---

a. Syr. idiom; lit. "from after times." Note the juxtaposition of ܥܠܡ which also means "eternal", with ܙܒܢ which
also means "temporal."

b. Compare this verse with ApEl 33:1-8, and see below
pp. 150-51. This verse is important for dating the Christian
portion of the Testament of Adam.

c. ApMos 39:2-3.

d. Lit. "After a long time of years."

e. Or "decay and dust." ܣܣܐ (maggot) also means "a period
of time."

f. ApMos 13:2b-3.

g. Following B.

---

¹ B: .

² Read with B: (B adds).

³ Read with B: .

⁴ B: omits; Kmosko suggests .

⁵ Read with B: .

were created in my image. And I do not leave you
to waste away in Sheol. For your sake I am born of
the virgin Mary. For your sake I taste death and
I enter the house of the dead. For your sake I make
a new heaven, and I am set over your posterity.

4   And after three days, while I am inside the tomb,
I will raise up the body which I received[a] from you.
And I will set you at the right hand of my divinity,
and I will m[ake] (you) a god as y[ou wanted].[b]

5   You have heard, my son Seth,[c] that there will be[d]
a flood,[e] and it will wash the whole earth because
of the daughters[f] of Cain, your brother, who out of

---

a.   Lit. "put on."

b.   Cf. ApMos 28:4 (A, B, and Arm), Gen 3:22, and Death of
Adam 22.

c.   ܒܪܫܝܬ also means "in the beginning", a remarkable play
on words. The line can be read: "I heard in the beginning",
or "you have heard, my son Seth." The diacritical mark and
word division here indicate the latter.

d.   Lit. "will come."

e.   Adam prophesies the flood to Seth in ApocAd 69:2-70:9,
and *Ant.* 1.2.3.

f.   MS F reads "house" (ܒܝܬ).

¹   6
²
³
⁴   7
⁵
---

¹B: .

²B: ‾.

³B is illegible here.

⁴B: .

⁵B: omits waw (conj.).

passion for Lebuda,[a] your sister, killed Abel, your
brother, in that sins had been created through Eve,
your mother. And after the flood, the years (remain-
ing) to the form of the world will be six thousand
years, and its end will be at that time.

6   And I, Seth, wrote this testament.[b] And my father
died, and they buried him at the east of paradise[c]
opposite the first city which was built on the earth,
which was named (the city of) Enoch.[d] And Adam
was borne to his grave by the angels and the powers
of heaven because he was created in the image of
God.[e] And the sun was darkened and the moon (also),[f]
and there was thick darkness for seven days.[g]

7   And we sealed the testament and we placed it in the
cave of treasures[h] along with the offerings which Adam
had taken out of paradise,[i] gold and myrrh and frankincense. And the sons of kings, the magi, will come

---

a. Cf. Gen. R. 22.7, PRE 21. See the discussion and
further references to the tradition concerning Cain's sister in
L. Ginzberg, *Legends of the Jews* (Philadelphia: Jewish Publication Society, 1928), vol. 1, pp. 108-09, vol. 5, pp. 138-39.

b. *Vita* 51:3, *Ant.* 1.2.3, and ApocAd 85:21.

c. *Vita* 45:2 and Jub 4:29.

d. Jub 4:9, *Ant.*1.2.2, and Gen 4:17.

e. ApMos 33, Death of Adam 39.

f. ApMos 34-5.

g. *Vita* 46:1.

h. See Budge, *Cave of Treasures*, pp. 72-3.

i. Cf. ApMos 29:5-6 where Adam takes crocus, nard,
calamus, and cinnamon from paradise.

ܩܘܒ̈ܠܬܐ ܠܗܘܢ ܗܘ̈ܝ ܕܐܠܗܐ
ܕܬܚܘܝܬܗ ܗܝܠܝܢ ܘܗܘܩܪܐ
ܕܫܢܝ̈ܗܝܢ ܘܐܝܠܝܢ: ܚܝ̈ܫ ܬܢܢ
ܕܐܡ̈ܪ ܐܝܟ ܗ̈ܘܘ.

---

[1] B: ܫܠܗ.

[2] B: ܚܫ̈ܬܐܒܘ.

[3] B: adds ܚܝ̈ܠ ܕܬܚܘܝܬܐ ܗܕܡ.

and get them and bring them to the son of God, to
Bethlehem of Judea, to the cave.

The End of the Testament of Our Father Adam

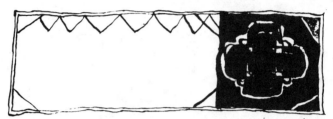

---

[1] Read .

Recension 2

(The Testament of Our Father Adam)

By the power of our Lord Jesus the Messiah we begin
to write this writing,[a] which is called a chronicle.
Amen.

The Hours of the Night[b]

1:1   The first hour of the night is the praise of the
      waters and of the demons. And in that hour of their
      praise they neither harm nor injure nor destroy any-
      thing until dismissed from their praises because a
      hidden power[c] of the maker of all binds them.

2   The second hour, pray for the sinner, the servant
      who writes,[d] is the praise of the fish and every
      creeping thing which is in the sea.

3   The third hour: the voice[e] of the depths and of fire
      from the depths. And from the fire below it is not
      lawful for a man to investigate in any way.

4   The fourth hour: the trishagion of the seraphim.
      Thus, my son, I used to hear, before I sinned, when

---

a. Or, "scripture."

b. This recension omits the hours of the day.

c. See below, 4:5.

d. This scribal gloss is written in very small letters.

e. Scribal error. Recensions 1 and 3 read ܠ (all) for
ܩܠ (voice).

---

[1] Read .

[2] Read .

[3] Read .

the seraphim were beating their wings with the fair
and pleasing sound of their trishagia. But after I
sinned and transgressed against the commandment, I
never again saw nor heard (anything) like that sound.

5   The fifth hour is the praise of the waters[a] which
    are above heaven. Thus, in the beginning,[b] I myself
    used to hear (both) angels (and) the sound of mighty
    waves which would raise praise to God[c] because a
    hidden signal from God was inspiring them.

6   The sixth[d] hour: the construction[e] of clouds and of
    the great fear occurring at midnight.

7   The seventh hour of the night: the repose of the
    powers and of every substance which is sleeping.
    And in that hour, the priest of God mixes the waters
    with oil and anoints whoever is not sleeping peace-
    fully.

8   The eighth hour is the praise to bring forth the
    grasses and seeds of the earth while the dew is
    descending on them from heaven.

9   The ninth hour: the worship of those angels who are
    standing before the throne of that majesty.

10 The tenth hour: the opening of the gates which the
    prayers of all that lives enter, and they worship and

---

a. The preceding word, "of the fish" has been crossed out.

b. Again, note the word play between "in the beginning"
and "my son Seth."

c. Recension 1 and 3 read "to the Creator."

d. The word "sixth" is crossed out in the MS.

e. Recension 3 reads "examination" (H: "petition").

---

[1] D:
[2] D: adds .

[3] Read with D: .

[4] D: .

[5] D: omits waw.

[6] D: .

they depart. For in that hour everything which our
race will ask from its maker is given to it in his
graciousness. And the wing(s) of the seraphim (are)
beating[a] and the roosters are crowing.

11 The eleventh hour: joy in all the earth while the
sun is rising from the paradise of the living God,
above his creation and shining forth upon all the
earth.

12 The twelfth hour: the waiting and silence imposed
on all the orders of fire and spirit until the
priests burn[b] incense to God. And at that time all
the orders and powers of his heaven are dismissed.

3:1 By Our Same First Father, Our Father Adam[c]

"I have heard, my son Seth,[d] that the Messiah is
coming from heaven and will be born of a virgin,[e]
working miracles and performing signs and great[f]
deeds, walking on the waves of the sea as upon boards
of wood,[g] rebuking the winds and they are silenced,
beckoning to the waves and they are still; also opening (the eyes of) the blind and cleansing the lepers,
and causing the deaf to hear. And the mute speak.
And he is casting out evil spirits, and driving out
demons, and restoring the dead to life, and raising
the buried from the midst of their graves.

2 Because of this the Messiah[h] spoke to me in paradise

---

a. The participle and its antecedent, "wing", are both
singular.

b. Syr. idiom, lit. "placing."

c. This is the first mention of Adam in rec. 2.

d. Or, "in the beginning."

e. MS D adds: "and will be with me and with my sons."

f. Reading with D.

g. Cp. Odes Sol 34:9-11.

h. Recension 1 and 3 read "God" for "Messiah."

---

[1] D: adds .

[2] D: omits .

[3] D: omits .

[4] D: omits .

[5] D: .

[6] D: .

[7] D: .

[8] D: .

[9] D: .

[10] D: .

[11] D: adds .

[12] D: .

[13] D: omits .

[14] D: .

[15] D: adds .

[16] D: .

[17] D: .

when I picked the fruit in which death was hiding.
And he said to me: 'Adam, do not fear. You wanted
to be a god;[a] I will make you (one). However, not
right now, but after a period of many years. I am
delivering up your body to the maggot and to the
worm[b] to eat,[c] and your bones to the worm.'[d]

3   And I said to him: 'Why, my Lord?' He said to me:
'Because you listened to the counsel of Eve, you
shall be food for the serpent,[e] and your children
after you. And after a short time my mercy will be
revealed to you because I created you in my own image.
And for your sake I will make a new earth for you.[f]
And I will be set over your children on it. And I
will ascend and sit at the right hand of my divinity,
and I will make you a god as I wanted.'"[g]

4   And I, Seth, said to my father, Adam:[h] "What is the
name of the fruit of which you ate?" He said to me:
"It was the fig,[i] my son, (which was) the gate by
which death entered into me and my posterity, and by

a.   Following D, C is corrupt.

b.   Or, "to decay and dust."

c.   Reading with D.

d.   Or, "to dust." Recension 2 here combines the readings
of 1 and 3.

e.   Note the striking paronomasia involving ܚܘܐ(Eve),
ܚܘܝܐ (serpent) and ܗܘܐ (to be). Cf. W. Wuellner, *Protocol of
the Third Colloquy of the Center for Hermeneutical Studies*
(Berkeley, 1975), p. 8.

f.   Recension 1 reads "new heaven."

g.   The diacritical mark indicates first person. Recension
1 has second person.

h.   This verse is found only in rec. 2.

i.   Cf. ApMos 20:4-5 and Gen. R. 15. See also Wuellner,
Protocol of the Third Colloquy, p. 9.

---

[1]D: adds .

[2]D: .

[3]D: .

[4]In D follows .

[5]D: .

[6]D: .

[7]D: adds .

[8]D: .

[9]D: .

[10]D: .

[11]D: adds .

[12]D: .

[13]D: omits the remainder of chapter three, and all of chapter four.

it life shall come to me and to my children (when) our
Lord shall become a man from the virgin and put on a
holy body[a] at the end of the ages.

5   I heard, my son, from the beginning that there will
     be[b] a flood, and it will despoil the whole earth.
     And after the flood all the years (remaining for) this
     world will be six thousand years. And at that time
     will come the destruction of this world.

6   After my father Adam died I, Seth, buried him,[c] I and
     my brother, at the east of paradise and I placed this
     testament in the cave of treasures until the present
     day.

     Also From the Testament of Our Father Adam

4:1 The heavenly powers, what they are like, and how each
     of their orders is occupied in service and in the plan
     which concerns this world. Listen, my beloved,[d]
     while they are set in array one order after another,[e]
     from the bottom until we reach those who carry our
     Lord Jesus the Messiah and bear him up. The lowest

---

a.   Following D; lit. "our Lord became man and will put
on a body from a holy virgin." In D the body is holy, while
in C the virgin is holy.

b.   Lit. "will come."

c.   The verb is plural.

d.   Plural; i.e., not likely Adam to Seth.

e.   Lit. "after its fellow."

2

3

[1]Read .

order is (that of) the angels.[a] And the plan has
been revealed to it by God concerning each and every
human being whom they are guarding, so that one angel
from this lowest order will accompany every single
human being who is in the world for his protection.
And this is its service.

2   The second order is (that of) the archangels. This
is the service: that they direct everything according to the plan of God, everything which is in this
creation, whether powers or animals, flying creatures
or creeping things, or fish, and to speak briefly
and in short, whatever (there) is in this creation,
aside from human beings, that they show concern for it
and guide it.

3   The third order, which is archons. This is its
service: that they move the air so that a cloud
rises from the ends of the earth, as (in) the words
of the prophet David, and rain descends upon the
earth.[b] And it makes all the changes of the air,
sometimes rain and sometimes snow and sometimes

---

a. For parallels to the order of angels, cf. Col 1:16,
Eph 1:21, 2En 20:1-4, TLev 3:7-8. However the closest parallels
are the angelologies of the Book of the Bee, chap. 5, the Hierarchy of pseudo-Dionysius the Areopagite, the opening lines of
the Cave of Treasures, and the Vision of Isaiah. See also
Letter to Diognetus 7:2.

b. Cf. 1Kgs 18:44f.

محوح لحكحذا. وحوح لحجغا. وهو بند محسلك
لحص. وحبلہ الهی لند ذتحسا ونحذا وحدثا
هلطغا لحذ حزز حنا حزز تهحب عملغنا. احذيہ
محجحسہ. محجحدذنهم ح بحذا. ح حسحنا   4
ونغحدذا محمحجنا .. هلغنا حم حبنعغا حزا بهہ
نسلا احزايج محجيحسہ. حبمحلم لحازجـــــ
دلا نصحبوم لحذبهم حزا لنا. مجلا سهحبحم   5

دلهم جننعنا. حنا حبلہ بند محم حب
احهزا حننا لهنا حجازذا. حز نحملك فلم حبحنوہ
نسدا عغا محبنا محهفحم اهو لہ لحذنا
حلہ. انا حلا قلم لحص ملا حالزهنا . حنا   6
حهم حلمحم لند نلحذا حلا بحلحم فلنا
حزحنحسم نحثذا .. هلغنا حم حبعنا حزا بهحم
محمنا احزايج محجيحسہ هنص. حبعلحلم
حلا حلنحم، ۱۵. بجنحم اهنا اححنا منلحہ
۲۱ ححذنا، ۵. محبم نحبحم حم احذا بحذنا
لند ابههہ لم لهم ملحا حللغا بحمحنا. خجبحم
هلم حلا لانحنعللم نبح ملانغا موہ ہ .

---

hail and sometimes dust and sometimes blood. And it
changes them. And these belong to this (order):[a]
thunder and the fire of lightning.

4 The fourth order, which is authorities. This is its
service: the administration of the lights, of the
sun and of the moon and of the stars.

5 The fifth order, which is the powers. This is its
service: to restrain the demons lest they destroy the
creation of God, because of their jealousy toward
human beings; because if the accursed nature of
demons was allowed to perform the desire of its will,
in one hour and a moment they would overthrow[b] all
creation. But[c] the divine strength stops them, in
that a guard is set against them lest they succeed in
accomplishing the desire of their will.

6 The sixth order, which is dominions. This is its
service: they are the ones who have authority over
kingdoms, and [in][d] their hands are victory and
defeat in battle. And this is so indicated[e] by (what
happened) to the Assyrian king. For when he rose up
against Jerusalem an angel came down and plundered the

---

a. Lit. "and his are they."

b. Compound present tense.

c. Following Kmosko's emendation.

d. Ibid.

e. Ibid.

The Testament of Adam

7

8

---

[1] Read ܡܣܒܪ.

[2] Read with the Peshitta ܐܠܗܝܢ.

[3] Read ܡܚܒ.

[4] Kmosko emends to ܚܕܪ.

[5] Read ܕܗܘܐ.

camp of the wicked (one). And in one moment one
hundred and eighty-five thousand died.[a]

7   And also the blessed Zechariah saw the angel[b] in
the likeness of a man riding upon a red horse which
was standing among the trees of the tabernacle,[c] and
after him (others on) white and red horses with lances
in their hands. And Judah the Maccabee[d] also saw the
angel when (he was) riding on the red horse which was
all decked out (in) trappings of gold.[e] Seeing him,
the camp of Antiochus the Wicked fled before him. And
wherever there is victory or defeat, these transmit
it[f] at a signal from the living God, who commands
them in the hour of battle.

8   These other orders, of thrones and seraphim and
cherubim, are the ones who stand before the majesty of
our Lord Jesus the Messiah and serve the throne of
his magnificence, glorifying (him) hourly with their
trishagia.[g] And the cherubim[h] bear his throne and

---

a.   Following Kmosko's emendation. Cf. 2Kgs 19:35 and
Isa 37:36.

b.   Cf. Zech 1:7-17.

c.   The phrase should be emended to read with the Peshiṭta
of Zech 1:8, "among the shady trees" (see text).

d.   Following Kmosko's emendation.

e.   Cf. 2Mac 3:24-6.

f.   Or, accepting Kmosko's emendation "bring it to pass."

g.   This phrase may presuppose an acquaintance with the
Horarium; see below pp. 146-48.

h.   Following Kmosko's emendation.

ܢ ܣܓܕܝܢ‸ ܗܕܟܐ ܕܝܢ ܠܟܝܠܘܝܘ ܕܥܢ ܡܬܥܠܝܢ
ܡܗܩܐ ܕܝܢ ܗܢܟܠܘ ܕܡܕܢܬ ܗܘܢܬܐ ܣܓܕܝܢ
ܘܐܘܪܚ ܐܘ ܥܕܬܐܐ. ܟܘܕ̈ܟ ܗܡܡܢܬܐܐ ܕܡܘܕܐ
ܠܡܝܠܗ ܕܡܠܐܟܐ ܕܕܘܡܐ ܢܠܟܝܐ ܥܠܘ ܚܣܟ
ܚܘܕܕ ܢܘ ܕܥܢ ܠܡܝܚܗܕ ܕܢܗܡܐܘܐܚܘ ܠܕܡ

honor (it) and keep the seals. And the seraphim
serve the inner chamber of our Lord, and the thrones
keep the gate of the holy of holies. This is, in
truth, the interpretation of the services of the plan
of the angels which (concerns) this world.

In the Strength of Our Lord's Help the End of the Writing,
        The Testament of Our Father Adam

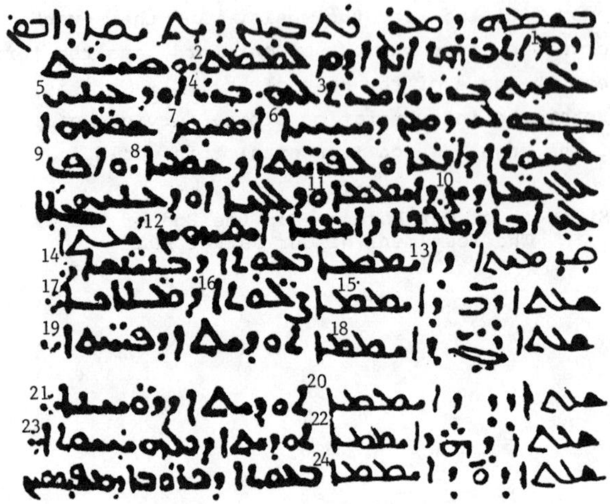

2:1

2

3

4

5

6

[1] E: [illegible]
G: [illegible]
H: [illegible] (omits [illegible]).

[2] E: [illegible]
G: [illegible]

[3] EG: [illegible]

[4] G: adds [illegible]

[5] EG: [illegible]

[6] E: adds [illegible]

[7] EG: [illegible]

[8] G: [illegible]

[9] E: [illegible]

[10] EG: omit [illegible]

[11] E: [illegible]
G: through haplography omits [illegible]

[12] E: [illegible]
H: omits [illegible]

[13] E: [illegible]

[14] G: adds [illegible]

[15] EH: [illegible] (H: adds [illegible]).
G: [illegible]

[16] E: omits [illegible]

[17] G: adds [illegible]

[18] E: [illegible]
G: [illegible]
H: [illegible]

[19] H: omits [illegible] and adds [illegible]

[20] EH: [illegible]
G: [illegible]

[21] EG: [illegible]
H: [illegible]

[22] EH: [illegible]
G: [illegible]

[23] E: [illegible]
H: [illegible]

[24] EH: [illegible]
G: [illegible]

Recension 3

2:1   In the Name of Our Lord We Write the
       Testament of Our Father Adam

I, Adam, was sick unto death and I called Seth, my
son, and said to him: "My son, he who formed me from
the dust[a] taught me to assign names to the beasts of
the earth and to the flying creatures of heaven,[b] and
he taught me[c] also about the hours of the day and of
the night, and revealed to me, the father of kings,[d]
what they are like. The first hour of the day: the
petition of human beings.

2   The 2nd[e] hour of the day: the prayers of the angels.[f]

3   The 3rd hour of the day: the praise of flying crea-
    tures.

4   The 4th hour of the day: the praise of the spiritual
    beings.[g]

5   The 5th hour of the day: the praise of every beast.[h]

6   The 6th hour of the day: the petition of the cheru-
    bim who intercede in behalf of the human race.

---

a. Lit. "my maker from the dust."

b. Cf. Jub 3:2.

c. Following EG.

d. Or, "of counsels."

e. The ordinals are here represented with arabic numerals
rather than being written out to reflect the character of the
Syriac text.

f. G adds "of light."

g. EG preserve the better reading: "of creeping things."
The reading above results from the confusion of ܪܚܫܐ (creeping
things) with ܪܘܚܢܐ (spiritual).

h. E reads "of all creeping things and of beasts."

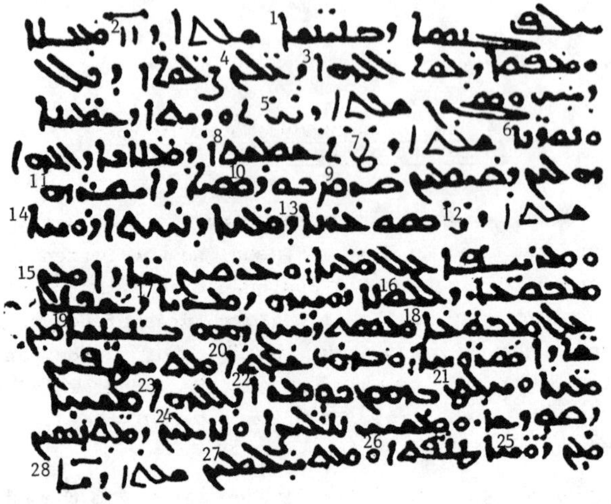

[Syriac manuscript text with interlinear verse/variant numbers 1–28, lines numbered 7, 8, 9, 10, 11 in the right margin.]

---

1 G: ⟨Syriac⟩.
 E: ⟨Syriac⟩ for ⟨Syriac⟩.

2 EH: ⟨Syriac⟩.
 G: ⟨Syriac⟩.

3 E: ⟨Syriac⟩.
 H: ⟨Syriac⟩.
 EH: omit remainder of verse.

4 G: ⟨Syriac⟩.

5 EH: ⟨Syriac⟩.
 G: ⟨Syriac⟩.

6 E: ⟨Syriac⟩.
 G: ⟨Syriac⟩.
 H: ⟨Syriac⟩.

7 EH: ⟨Syriac⟩.
 G: ⟨Syriac⟩.

8 E: ⟨Syriac⟩.

9 H: ⟨Syriac⟩ (omits remainder of verse).

10 G: ⟨Syriac⟩.

11 E: ⟨Syriac⟩.

12 EH: ⟨Syriac⟩.
 G: ⟨Syriac⟩.

13 EH: ⟨Syriac⟩.

14 H: ⟨Syriac⟩.

15 EG: omit ⟨Syriac⟩.

16 EH: omit ⟨Syriac⟩.
 G: ⟨Syriac⟩.

17 G: reads ⟨Syriac⟩ for ⟨Syriac⟩.

18 G: adds ⟨Syriac⟩.

19 G: adds ⟨Syriac⟩.

20 G: ⟨Syriac⟩.
 H: ⟨Syriac⟩.

21 E: ⟨Syriac⟩.

22 EGH: ⟨Syriac⟩.

23 EG: omit ⟨Syriac⟩.

24 G: ⟨Syriac⟩.
 H: ⟨Syriac⟩.

25 EG: add ⟨Syriac⟩.

26 E: omits ⟨Syriac⟩.

27 G: ⟨Syriac⟩.

28 E: ⟨Syriac⟩.
 G: ⟨Syriac⟩.
 H: ⟨Syriac⟩.

7   The 7th hour: the entry and exit from before God,
    when the prayers of all that lives enter and worship.

8   The 8th hour: the praise of the heavenly and fiery
    beings.[a]

9   The 9th hour: the worship[b] of the angels of God, the
    ones who stand before the throne of his magnificence.

10 The 10th hour: the visitation of the waters, when
    the spirit is descending and brooding over the waters
    and the demons are fleeing from the fountains. And if
    the spirit of the Lord did not settle over the
    fountains, human beings would be injured by the wicked
    demons. And in that hour the waters are taken up and
    the priest of God mixes them with consecrated oil and
    anoints the afflicted and those who are assailed by
    unclean spirits, and they are healed.

11 The 11th hour: the exultation and joy of the
    righteous.[c]

-----

    a. E reads "of heaven and earth and fiery beings"; G:
"of sun and of fire"; H: "of heaven and fire."

    b. E reads "hymn."

    c. The Greek reads "of the elect."

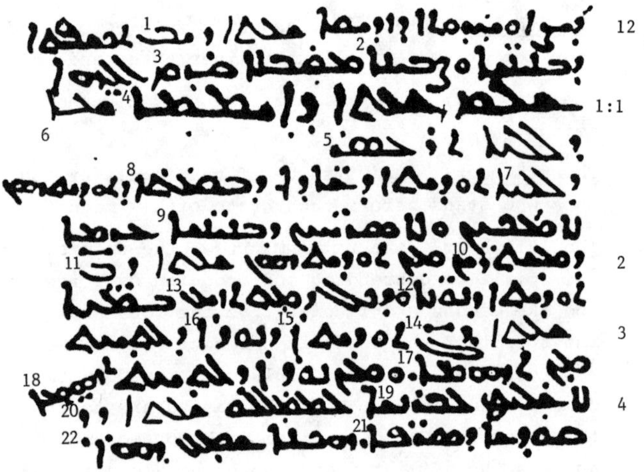

---

[1] E: [Syriac].
G: [Syriac].
H: [Syriac].

[2] H: [Syriac].
EG: [Syriac] for [Syriac].

[3] G: [Syriac].

[4] EGH: omit [Syriac]...[Syriac].

[5] E: [Syriac].
G: [Syriac].
H: [Syriac].

[6] Read with EH: [Syriac].
G: [Syriac].

[7] EG: omit.

[8] GH: [Syriac].

[9] E: [Syriac].
G: [Syriac].
H: reads [Syriac] for [Syriac] and adds [Syriac].

[10] G: [Syriac].
E: [Syriac].

[11] EH: [Syriac].
G: [Syriac].

[12] H: omits remainder of verse.

[13] E: [Syriac].
G: [Syriac].

[14] E: [Syriac].
G: [Syriac].
H: [Syriac].

[15] EG: add [Syriac].
H: adds [Syriac] and omits the remainder of this verse.

[16] E: [Syriac].
G: [Syriac].

[17] E: [Syriac] and omits the remainder of this verse.

[18] EG: omit [Syriac]...[Syriac].

[19] G: [Syriac].

[20] EH: [Syriac].
G: [Syriac].

[21] H: the remainder of the verse reads [Syriac].

[22] E: [Syriac].
G: [Syriac] for [Syriac].

12   The 12th hour: the supplication of human beings to[a]
     the gracious will which is with[b] God.

              The End of the Hours of the Day

1:1   The Twelve Hours of the Night

     [The first hour] of the night: the praise of the
     demons who, while they shout their praise,[c] neither
     harm nor injure any human being until released from
     their praise.

2   The 2nd hour: the praise of the fish and of all that
     moves[d] in the waters.[e]

3   The 3rd hour: the praise of the fire beneath the
     deep. And of the fire which is beneath the depths
     it is not lawful for a man to speak.

4   The 4th hour: The trishagion of the seraphim. Thus,
     I[f] used to hear in paradise before I sinned, but after

---

a.   Reading with EGH.

b.   Reading with G.

     c.   Lit. "in the shouting of their praise." GH read "in
the hour of their praise."

d.   G reads "all that lives."

     e.   EGH agree with the Greek and include "dragons" in
this hour.

f.   MS H gives third person singular.

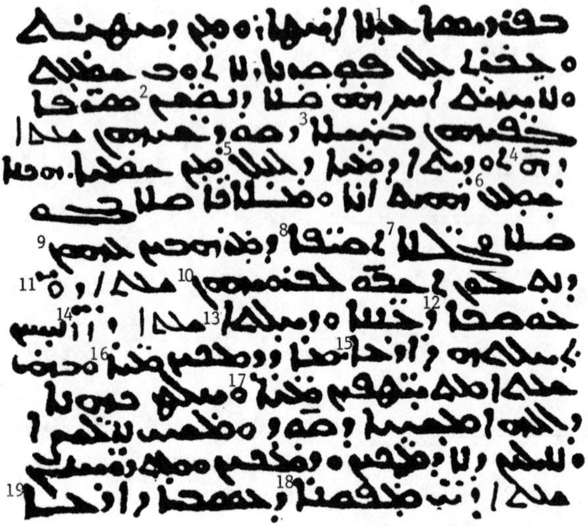

[Syriac text, lines marked with superscript note numbers 1–19 and verse numbers 5, 6, 7, 8 in the right margin]

---

[1] G: .

[2] E: .
G: .

[3] EG: .

[4] EH: .
G: .

[5] E: and omits following .

[6] E: .

[7] EG:
(E:).

[8] E: .
H: omits .

[9] EGH: .

[10] E: .
G: .

[11] EH: .
G: .

[12] G: .
H: .

[13] E: adds .

[14] EH: .
G: .

[15] E:
G: .
H: .

[16] G: .
H: completes the verse with
E: completes this verse with
[17] G: completes this verse with
[18] E: .
G: .
H: .

[19] E: for .
H: omits and adds

I sinned and transgressed against the commandment, I
no longer heard or saw (anything) like that sound of
the seraphim beating their wings with the force[a] of
their trishagia.

5   The 5th hour: the praise of the waters which are
     above heaven. Thus I myself used to hear with the
     angels the sound within a sound[b] and mighty waves[c]
     that would inspire them[d] to raise a (hymn of) praise
     to their Creator.

6   The 6th hour: the investigation[e] of clouds and of
     fear.

7   The 7th hour: the [powers][f] of the earth are resting
     when the waters are sleeping. And in that hour the
     waters are taken up and the priest of God mixes
     consecrated oil and anoints the afflicted and those
     who are not sleeping[g] and they sleep and are relieved.

8   The 8th hour: the springing forth of the grass of
     the earth.[h]

---

a. EG read "sound".

b. Or, "Thus I myself used to hear both the angels (and)
the sound within a sound".

c. E reads "wheels"; see p. 55, n. a.

d. I.e., the wheels.

e. Scribal error mistaking ܪܟܘܒܐ (composition) for ܥܩܒܬܐ
(investigation). H reads "petition".

f. Following GH, which preserve the better reading. F is
corrupt. In E the scribe has mistaken ܚܝܠܘܬܐ (powers) for
ܚܝܘܬܐ (beasts), a mistake which is repeated in the Greek version.

g. Rec. 3 combines the readings of rec. 1, "anoints the
afflicted", and rec. 2, "anoints those who are not sleeping".

h. MS H adds "when the dew (is) descending upon it",
thus supporting the reading of rec. 1 and 2.

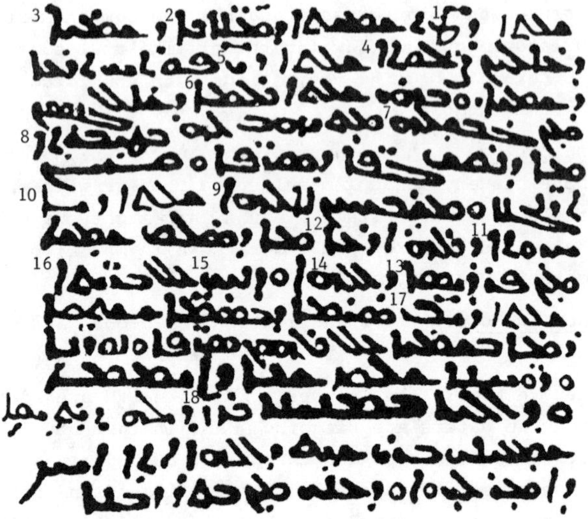

[Syriac text, verses 9–12 and 3:1, with superscript verse/line numbers]

---

¹EH: .
   G: .

²E: .

³GH: omit.

⁴E:
   GH:
    (H:)

⁵E: reads for this hour
   G: .
   H: reads for this hour
⁶G: for).

⁷G: adds .

⁸G: .

⁹G:
¹⁰E: .
   G: .
   H: .

¹¹H: .

¹²E: .
   G: .

¹³EH: (H: .

¹⁴E: .

¹⁵H: .

¹⁶E: .
   G: .

¹⁷E: .
   G: .
   H: .

¹⁸E:
   G:
   H: -

9   <u>The 9th hour</u>: the worship of the angels of heaven who bring in the prayers.[a]

10   <u>The 10th hour</u>: (the) opening of the gate of heaven. And in that hour whatever our race asks from its maker is given to it in graciousness when the wings of the seraphim are beating,[b] and the roosters are crowing and glorifying God.

11   <u>The 11th hour</u>: the joy of all the earth while the sun is rising from the paradise of God and shining forth upon creation.[c]

12   <u>The 12th hour</u>: the burning of incense and the silence imposed in heaven on all the seraphim and the fiery and spiritual (beings)."

The End of the Hours of the Day and of the Night
in Number <u>24</u>

3:1   <u>His Testament</u>

"Listen to me, my son Seth,[d] for God is coming after a long time,[e] just as he told me and taught me.

---

a. E reads "the praise of all the angels of heaven, and the prayers enter in before God when the seraphim beat their wings and the rooster crows."

b. The participle is singular.

c. E adds "and on every desert place."

d. Written as one word, ܒܪܝܫܝܬ, also means "in the beginning."

e. Lit. "from after times."

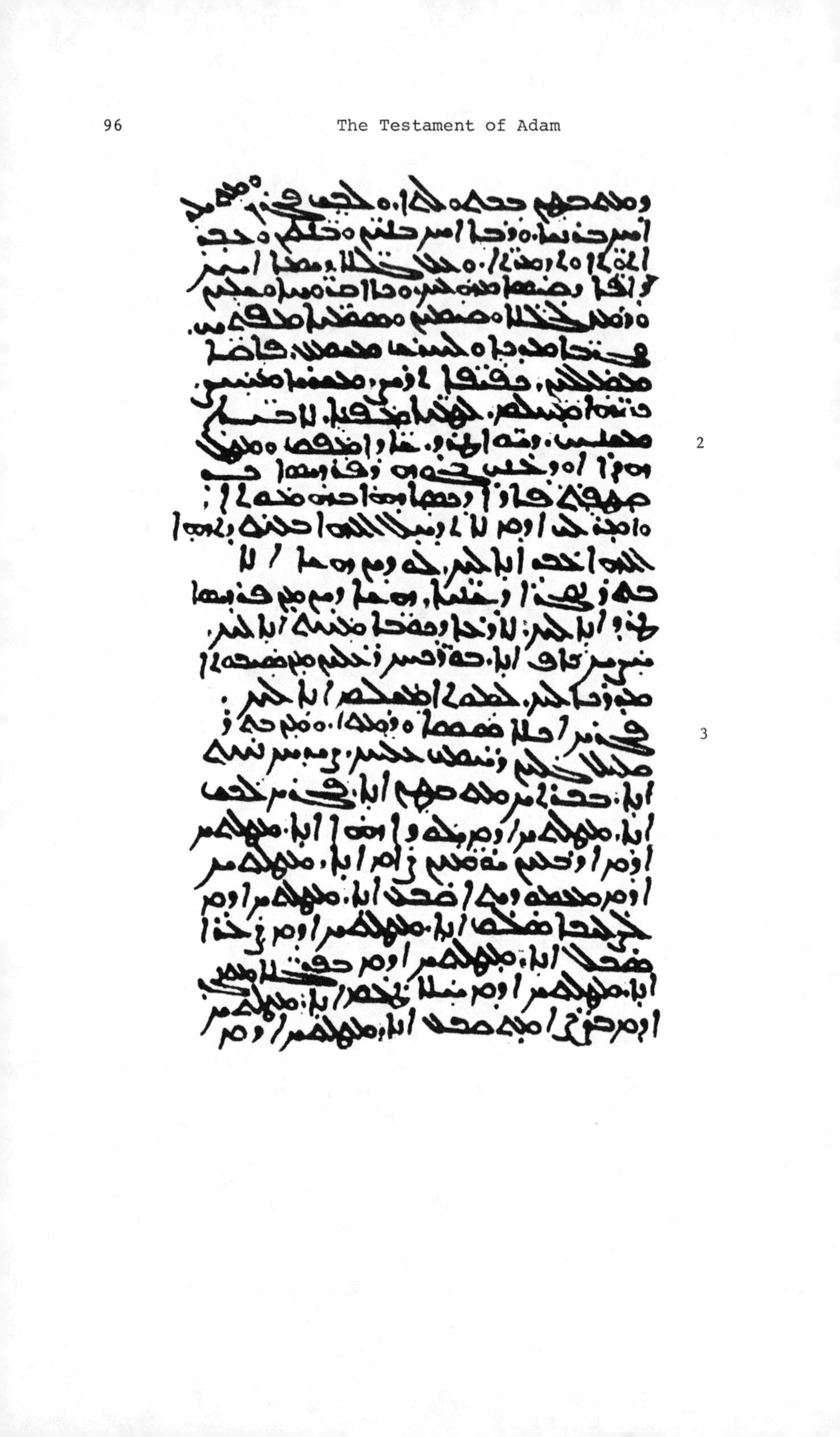

2

3

Who, conceived by a virgin, shall put on our body, being born as a human being, and growing up like our sons and daughters, and performing signs and wonders, and walking on the waves of the sea as (on) boards of wood, rebuking the winds and they are silenced, beckoning to the waves and they stand still; also opening (the eyes of) the blind and cleansing the lepers, and causing the deaf to hear; the mute speak; the hunchbacked are straightened up;[a] strengthening the paralyzed, healing the sick, turning those who err, finding the lost, driving out evil spirits, casting out demons.

2   And on this account he taught me in the midst of paradise when I picked the fruit in which death was hiding. And he said to me, 'Adam, do not fear. A god you desired to be; a god I will make you. However, not right now but after a space of (many) years. Right now[b] I (am going to) drive you from paradise, and I will bring you down into the earth of thorns. Your back I will bend (and) your knees will quake from old age overtaking you. I am delivering you up to death. The maggot and worm[c] will devour your body.

3   And after a short time my mercy (will be) revealed to you: I will go down to you. I will be conceived within your daughter. Your body I will put on. For your sake, Adam, I become an infant. For your sake, Adam, I fast for forty days. For your sake, Adam, I receive baptism. For your sake, Adam, I ascend the cross. For your sake, Adam, I suffer shame. For your sake, Adam, I am scourged with whips. For your sake, Adam, I taste vinegar. For your sake, Adam, I am transfixed with nails. For your sake, Adam, I am

---

a. Plural subject with singular passive participle.

b. "Right now . . . overtaking you" is found only in rec. 3.

c. Or, "decay and dust."

4

5

thrust through with a lance. For your sake, Adam,
the heavenly places are shaken. For your sake, Adam,
I darken the sun. For your sake, Adam, I roll up
heaven. For your sake, Adam, I provoke the powers.
For your sake, Adam, I open the tomb. For your sake,
Adam, I strip the earth bare. For your sake, Adam,
I make a new heaven. For your sake, Adam, I create a
new earth.[a]

(A blank space of nine lines)

4   And after three days, while I am in the tomb, I will
    raise up the body which I received from you. And I
    will raise it up and I will set it at the right hand
    of my divinity. And I will make you a god as you
    desired.' And you also, my son Seth,[b] (must) keep
    the commandments of God and not despise his words
    because he is going to come! And being seized by
    evil and wicked human beings and numbered among evil-
    doers, he will ascend the cross and he will be slain
    and he will be buried. And he will raise up the body
    which he received[c] from you and he will set it at the
    right hand.

5   Hear me, my son Seth, because a flood is coming and
    will wash the whole earth because of the house[d] of
    Cain, your brother, an evil man,[e] who killed his
    brother out of passion for Lubia, his sister. And
    after the flood, the years (remaining) until the end
    of the world are ten thousand weeks of years,[f] and

---

a. Rec. 3 combines the readings of 1 and 2.

b. The rest of this verse, to "And he will raise up", is
found only in rec. 3. Note the shift from participles to
imperfects.

c. Rec. 3 combines the readings of 1 and 2.

d. Rec. 1 reads "daughters (ܒܢܬ)."

e. The MS gives the plural under the influence of the
collective noun.

f. Rec. 1 and 2 read "six thousand years."

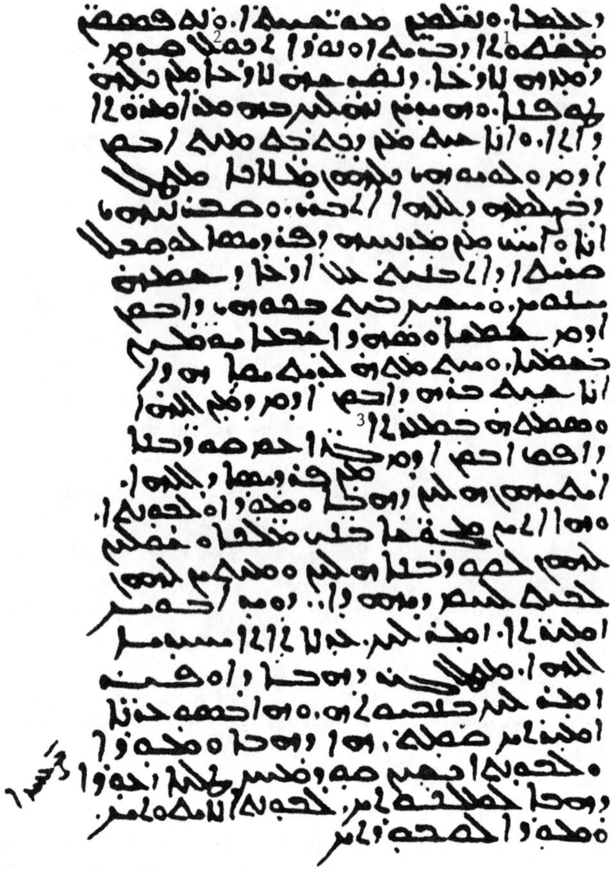

[Syriac text, 24 lines of manuscript, with verse numbers 6, 7, 8 in the right margin]

6

7

8

---

[1] Read ܡܚܘܝܬܐ.

[2] Read with Kmosko ܟܝܘܒܐ.

[3] Read with Kmosko ܚܕܬܐ.

(then) will be the end of the world. Then the calcu-
lations will cease and for created things, the threads
(of life) will be cut. And fire will devour the earth
before his sign,[a] that he may sanctify the earth from
every flood. And then the Lord of Lords who is coming,
will walk upon it."

6   And I Seth, am (the one) who wrote (it). Our father
Adam died and all the angels bore him (to his grave)
because he was created in the image of God. We buried
him, my brothers and I, at the east of paradise,
opposite the [first][b] city which was built on the
earth, which was named (the city of) Enoch. And
lamentation for our father Adam darkened the sun and
the moon in heaven for seven days.

7   And I sealed this testament, and I, Seth, the son of
our father Adam, who (came) from God,[c] placed it in
the cave of treasures with the offerings which our
father Adam had taken out of the paradise of God.
These are gold and myrrh and frankincense. And
behold, the Magi are coming, the sons of kings, and
they will take up these offerings and will bring them
to Bethlehem of Judea.

8   David, your father, sang psalms to you,[d] before you
came, only begotten God. For he sang to you (of) the
gold of Ophir in his prophecy.[e] And behold, the literal
sense (of) your psalm has stood firm. Behold, gold and
myrrh and frankincense are heaped before you, a little
child. Gold for your royalty, frankincense for your
(divine) substance, and myrrh for your burial.[f]

---

a.   Cf. Mt 24:3, 30.

b.   Following rec. 1 and 2.

c.   Cf. Lk 3:39.

d.   This verse, found only in MS F, is elsewhere attributed
to Ephraem Syrus. See below pp. 102-03.

e.   Cf. Ps 45:9.

f.   The marginal note reads: "in the codex is strength."

In recension 1, apart from differences of spelling, abbreviation and pointing, there are only five variants between manuscripts A and B, and all of these are minor. This is a remarkable agreement between two manuscripts written seven hundred years apart, and demonstrates that the two are closely related. By way of contrast, there is a substantially larger number of variants between manuscripts C and D than between A and B, even though the historical evidence for a close relationship between them is much stronger than in the case of A and B. Both C and D were copied in the vicinity of Mosul; C was copied in 1702, D in 1709. The contents of both are the same and occur in exactly the same order up to that point where C ends. The single exception to this is that D, the younger of the two manuscripts, omits the hours of the night, which are found in C. Manuscript D is the only Syriac manuscript of the Testament of Adam to omit the Horarium completely.[25]

Given the close historical relationship of time and place between C and D, the sizeable number of variants is probably due to a freer treatment accorded to the tradition in recension 2 than in recension 1, as evidenced by the expansive nature of both C and D in the Testament of Adam. This tendency is apparent both in scribal interjections,[26] and in additions to the text itself.[27] Also, the long additional section on the orders of angels is found only in recension 2. However, while recension 2 manifests an expansive tendency in those portions of the text which are represented, it also omits several blocks of the tradition found in recensions 1 and 3.[28] The conclusion to be drawn from all of this is that recension 2 has experienced a higher level of editorial activity, consisting of both additions and deletions, than have recensions 1 and 3.

Recension 3 is generally more expanded than recension 1, though again, this is true only of those sections which the several manuscripts have in common, since in recension 3 only manuscript F contains the Prophecy of Adam to Seth. An examination of the variants found among the hours of the night reveals that the four manuscripts of recension 3 tend to agree slightly with the readings of recension 2 against those of recension 1.[29] However, in the Prophecy, the readings agree stikingly with recension 1 against recension 2 and at one point the readings

of 1 and 2 are combined.[30] This would indicate that while
recension 3 has not been overly influenced by recension 1 in
the hours of the night, in the Prophecy it has at least been
influenced by recension 1, and has possibly even been added to
manuscript F from it.[31] This does not include the final verse
of F which is an addition taken from the writings of Ephraem
Syrus.[32]

It is unlikely that recension 3 witnesses an original of
the Testament of Adam which contained only the Horarium, since
two of the three manuscripts which omit the Prophecy clearly
indicate that the Horarium has been excerpted from a larger
work,[33] and since all the versions except the Greek also contain
the Prophecy. Further, as Kmosko and Reinink have pointed out,
recension 3 demonstrates by its expansions and errors that it
is secondary to recension 1.[34] The most notable of the errors
is the confusion at 2:7 of ܚܝܠܘܬܐ (powers) for ܚܝܘܬܐ (beasts)
in manuscript E of recension 3, an error which is repeated in
the Greek. Other errors occur at 2:4, ܒܚܝܠܐ (with the force)
for ܒܩܠܐ (with the sound), and 2:6, ܥܩܒܐ (investigation) for
ܪܘܟܒܐ (composition). Notable expansions occur at 1:1, 3:2,
3:3, 3:4, 3:5, and 3:8. Also, the Christian elements of the
Prophecy in recension 3 have been expanded excessively and the
order of the hours has been changed to put the day first, following the Roman custom. A comparison of fifty-three major
variants between the three recensions reveals that:

1. Recensions 1 and 2 agree against 3 -- 19 times
2. Recensions 1 and 3 agree against 2 -- 19 times
3. Recensions 2 and 3 agree against 1 -- 12 times
4. All three recensions differ -- 3 times
5. Recension 2 combines 1 and 3 -- 2 times
6. Recension 3 combines 1 and 2 -- 2 times
7. Recension 1 never combines 2 and 3

These results, in addition to the information above, indicate
two things: first, that recensions 2 and 3 are secondary to
recension 1, since 1 is most often the middle term and never
combines 2 and 3; second, that the three recensions have
already become substantially mixed and any of the three may
preserve the original reading at a given point, the overall
priority of recension 1 notwithstanding. Finally, the

relationship of the eight Syriac manuscripts to each other and
to the Syriac autograph may be expressed thus:

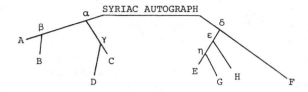

A stylistic feature common to all eight manuscripts is the
regular employment of the present participle, without an auxiliary verb or enclitic pronoun, for the present tense. Otherwise the texts offer few stylistic peculiarities.

The biblical orientation of the Syriac text is undeniable.
The story of Genesis 1-6 is worked into the very fiber of the
document. The angelology and demonology, the Old and New Testament allusions,   and the creation motif heavily influenced
by Genesis 1 disclose that the Horarium from the Testament of
Adam was composed squarely within the biblical tradition.[35]

CHAPTER IV

THE GREEK TESTAMENT OF ADAM

The hours of the day and night, which constitute chapters
one and two of the Syriac Testament of Adam, are extant in
Greek in two forms. The first form is witnessed by four manuscripts from the Bibliothèque Nationale in Paris (ABCD), one
from the Deutsche Staadtbibliothek in Berlin (E) and one from
the Collection of the University of Bonn (F). In four of these
six manuscripts the hours of the day and night form one chapter
in a larger work of astrological and magical speculations
attributed to Apollonius of Tyana and entitled *Apotelesmata*.[1]
The account of the hours in this recension is shorter than in
the Syriac text and all references to the figure of Adam are
missing. The text of manuscript A was first published in
1893 by M. R. James.[2] Portions of Paris manuscript 2316 (C)
were published by R. Reitzenstein in 1904.[3] All four Paris
manuscripts were edited by F. Nau, who published an eclectic
text in 1907.[4] The Berlin manuscript (E) was published by
F. Boll in 1908.[5] Portions of the Bonn manuscript including
the Horarium were published by A. Delatte in 1927.[6] In order
to facilitate the use of earlier literature, the numeration
and sigla of F. Nau have been preserved where possible. The
six manuscripts are:

A - Paris Greek manuscript 2419, a paper codex of the
late fifteenth or early sixteenth century. This
manuscript measures 410 x 310 mm and is written in
an inelegant hand. It is crowded, averaging
thirty-eight lines per page in a single column.
The hours of the day and night appear on folio
247[b]. This is the only one of the six Greek manuscripts that assigns Hebrew names to the hours.
A key for deciphering the Hebrew letters and other
symbols is provided by Delatte, *Anecdota Atheniensia*,
p. 446.

B - Paris supplemental Greek manuscript 1148, a paper
    codex copied between A.D. 1539 and A.D. 1542. It
    contains 231 folios and measures 240 x 175 mm with
    approximately 22 lines per page. The hours of the
    day and night appear on folios 37^b-40^b. This manu-
    script served as the base text for Nau's edition
    of 1907. It seems, however, to be dependent on
    manuscript E, which was unknown to Nau.[7]

C - Paris Greek manuscript 2316 is a paper codex of the
    fifteenth century. This manuscript has 459 folios,
    measuring 215 x 145 mm, with 26 lines per page
    and is written in an inelegant hand. The hours of
    the day and night appear on folios 324^b- 325^b. In
    this manuscript the hours are found independent of
    any connection with Apollonius of Tyana or his
    Apotelesmata.

D - Paris supplemental Greek manuscript 20 is a paper
    codex of the seventeenth century and is the latest
    of the six manuscripts. It is written in a very
    beautiful hand averaging 30 lines per page with
    marginalia in Latin and is a copy of MS 2419 (A)
    made by Ishmael Bullialdo. The hours of the day and
    night are found on folios 170^a-171^a. This manu-
    script leaves blank spaces at most of those points
    in the hours of the day and night where the parent
    manuscript, Paris 2419 (A), had Hebrew letters,
    although Hebrew letters have been copied in other
    chapters.[8]

E - Berlin Greek manuscript 173 is a paper codex of the
    late fifteenth century containing 204 folios and
    measuring 203 x 144 mm. The hours of the day and
    night are found in folios 73^a-74^a. This manuscript
    is certainly a genealogical predecessor if not
    indeed the actual parent of the Paris MS 1148 (B).

F - Codex Bononiensis Universitatis 3632 is a paper
    codex copied in the fifteenth century by John of
    Aron. It contains 475 folios and measures 296 x
    219 mm. The Horarium is found on folio 359^b.

This manuscript was unknown to F. Nau and was not
used in his 1907 edition of the Greek text.

In the following edition of the Greek text one manuscript
is employed as a base text; variant readings from the other
five are recorded in footnotes. This method is preferable
since it focuses study on an actual text rather than on one
that is hypothetical and eclectic. Manuscript A is used as
the base text for several reasons. It was the first discovered and has been the most discussed of the six manuscripts.
Also, it is the sole witness to the so-called Hebrew names
attributed to each hour. Since much has been made of these
Hebrew names in relation to the problems of original language,[9] it is well to have manuscript A before us. Finally,
manuscript A, though not the oldest, is generally the least
expanded of the six manuscripts.

The second form in which the hours of the day are found
in Greek is in a citation from the Byzantine chronicler
George Cedrenus (11th century) which is much abbreviated and
gives the distinct impression of being a summary or paraphrase. Although Cedrenus attributes the Horarium to Adam,
he lists only the hours of the day.[10]

In the Greek text below, underscoring indicates rubrication; in the English translation underscoring indicates
those words written in the Greek text in Hebrew characters.
The Hebrew words in the Greek text do not employ final forms
(i.e. ך, ף, ם, etc.) consequently these are not used below.
Hebrew letters found in the text have been transliterated in
the English translation, followed by the English meaning in
brackets where the meaning is ascertainable. The horizontal
stroke beneath some Hebrew letters is equivalent to the Greek
alpha (a, or ā).[11]

Although the Greek manuscripts are full of abbreviated
endings these have been spelled out in full below since the
abbreviations cannot be reproduced in printed form. Variants
involving ν-movable have not been noted. Parentheses in the
English translation indicate words demanded by good English;
brackets indicate editorial insertions beyond those required
for English sense. The text of Cedrenus' *Compendium* is taken
from I. Bekker's edition in *Corpus Scriptorum Historiae*

Byzantinae.[12]   The texts of manuscripts A, B, C and D are
taken from photographs graciously provided by the authorities
of the Bibliothèque Nationale; the text of manuscript E is
taken from the published edition of F. Boll;[13] and the text
of manuscript F is from the published edition of A. Delatte.[14]

Greek Manuscripts of the Testament of Adam

MS	Catalogue No.	Folios	Date
A	Paris 2419	247^b	late 15th cent.
B	Paris Suppl 1148	37^b-40^b	16th cent.
C	Paris 2316	324^b-325^b	15th cent.
D	Paris Suppl 20	170^a-171^a	17th cent.
E	Berlin 173	73^a-74^a	15th cent.
F	Bonn 3632	359^b	15th cent.

MS Paris 2419 f. 247[b]

Ὀνομασίαι ὡρῶν ἡμερινῶν[1]

1   Ὥρα α΄[2] καλεῖται[3] אֵיזֶכּ[4] ῷ[5] ἀγαθόν[6] ἐστι[7] προσεύχεσθαι.[8]

2   Ὥρα β΄[9] καλεῖται[10] בַּנוֹחוּרִיש[11] ἐν ῷ[12] εὔχαι[13] τῶν ἀγγέλων
    καὶ ὕμνοι.[14]

3   Ὥρα γ΄[15] καλεῖται אוּרבְנַדשׁוּ[16] ἐν ῷ[17] εὐχαριστοῦσιν[18] τὰ
    πετεινὰ τῷ θεῷ.[19] ἐν αὐτῇ τῇ ὥρᾳ[20] ἀποτελεῖται[21] πᾶν
    στοιχεῖον[22] אוּרבְנַא.[23]

---

[1]B: περὶ τῶν ὡρὸν τῆς γ(ῆς?)
ὡλοῦντ᾽ ὦ τί ἔργον ποιεῖ
ἑκάστη ὥρα.
  C: περὶ τῶν ὀνομάτων τῶν ὁρῶν
  τῆς ἡμέρας.
  E: Περὶ τῶν ὡρῶν τῆς ἡμέρας
  πῶς καλοῦνται καὶ τί ἔργον
  ποιεῖ ἑκάστη ὥρα.
  F: ἡμέρον.
James mistook ὡρῶν for ιβ΄.

[2]BE: Ἡ πρώτη ὥρα τῆς ἡμέρας.

[3]C: καλεῖτε.

[4]BCEF: ιαἐκ.
  C: adds καλεῖται.
  D: omits.

[5]BE: ἐν αὐτῇ τῇ ὥρᾳ (B: τῷ for
ὥρᾳ).
  C: ἐν ταύτῃ τῇ ὥρᾳ.
  F: omits.

[6]C: καλόν.

[7]BCE: add τοῖς ἀνθρώποις.

[8]F: προσευχῆς.

[9]BE: ἡ β΄ ὥρα τῆς ἡμέρας.

[10]B: καλλῆται.

[11]BE: ναουρᾶν.
  C: νανουρίς.
  D: omits.
  F: γανουκῆς.

[12]BCE: ἐν αὐτῇ (C: ταύτῃ) τῇ ὥρᾳ.
  F: omits ἐν ῷ.

[13]B: εὔλαί.

[14]BCE: καὶ (B adds μί) ὕμνοι τῶν
ἀγγέλων.
  F: εὐχῆς ἀμπέλων καὶ οἶκον.

[15]BE: ἡ τρίτη ὥρα.

[16]BE: χαρσϊάρω.
  C: οὐχοσιούρ.
  D: omits name.
  F: οὐχανσιούρ.

[17]BCE: ἐν αὐτῇ (C: ταύτῇ) τῇ ὥρᾳ.

[18]B: εὐχαριστῶσιν.
  BE: add πάντα.

[19]BCE: τὸν θεόν (BE add καί).

[20]C: ἐν ταύτῃ ὥρᾳ.
  F: τὴν αὐτὴν ὥραν.
  BE: omit.

[21]F: ἀποτελή.
  BE: add ἐν αὐτῇ.

[22]B: στοιχοῖον.
  C: στιχοῖον.

[23]B: τῶν ὀρέων.
  CE: τῶν ὄρνεων.
  DF: ὄρνεων.

The Greek Testament of Adam

The Names of the Hours of the Day

1   The 1st[a] hour is called 'y'hk [prayer][b] (in)
     which it is good to pray.

2   The 2nd hour is called nnwtwyś in which
     (there are) prayers and hymns of angels.

3   The 3rd hour is called 'wrndśw [talk like a
     bird][c] in which the birds give thanks to God.
     In the same hour every spell (pertaining to)
     'wrn'w [birds][d] is conjured.[e]

---

a.   The ordinals here and below are rendered with numbers
rather than letters to better reflect the character of the Greek
text. This is also characteristic of Syriac recension 3, with
which the Greek shares many common features.

b.   It will become increasingly clear below that the Hebrew
names in this text are not Hebrew at all, but where decipherable
they turn out to be Greek words written in Hebrew characters.
The form here is probably a corruption of εὐχή, "prayer." With
the exception of 1:1, 1:3, and 1:11, the names of the hours have
resisted satisfactory translation.

c.   I.e., ὀρνιάζω, or less probably οὐρανίζω, "to reach to
heaven."

d.   I.e., ὀρέων, as in the other five MSS. Note that D
offers a Greek word for the Hebrew of A.

e.   In late Byzantine texts, ἀποτελεῖν and στοιχεῖον, with
their cognates are technical terms in the practice of magic and
astrology, especially in the creation of talismans. For an
excellent exposition of the evidence see C. Blum, "The Meaning
of στοιχεῖον and its Derivates in the Byzantine Age," *Eranos* 44
(1946) 315-25. For other references see also E. A. Sophocles,
Greek Lexicon of the Roman and Byzantine Periods (Cambridge:
Harvard University Press, 1914), pp. 1012f.

4   "Ωρα δ'[1] καλεῖται[2] שׁלכן[3] ἐν ᾗ[4] εὐχαριστοῦσιν[5] πάντα τά
      ποιήματα[6] τῷ θεῷ·[7] ἐν ᾗ στοιχειοῦνται[8]
      דרכובנשׁ : אורפיישׁ : שׁכורפיאורי καὶ πάντα τὰ ἰοβόλα.[9]

5   "Ωρα ε'[10] καλεῖται שׁעלם[11] ἐν ᾗ[12] αἰνεῖ πᾶν ζῷον τὸν θεόν·
      ὅτε[13] ἀποτελεῖται[14] πᾶν מטרבפון.[15]

6   "Ωρα ς'[16] καλεῖται שׁכמול[17] ᾗ[18] δυσωποῦσιν[19] τὰ χερουβίμ
      τὸν θεὸν ὑπὲρ[20] ἀνθρώπων.[21]

---

[1]BE: ἡ τετάρτη ὥρα.

[2]C: καλῆται.

[3]BEF: σλάχνε.
 C: σπλάχνε.
 D: omits.

[4]BE: ἐν αὐτῇ τῇ ὥρᾳ.
 C: ἐν ταύτῃ γῇ ὥρᾳ.
 F: omits ἐν ᾗ.

[5]B: εὐχαριστῦ.
 C: εὐχαριστῶσι.
 F: εὐαρεστοῦσι.

[6]B: καὶ περὶ τούτου ποιήμετα.

[7]BCEF: τὸν θεόν.

[8]BCE: ἐν ταύτῃ τῇ (B omits τῇ)
 ὥρᾳ ἀποτελεῖται πᾶν στοιχεῖον (C: στοιχίον.)
 F: ἐν ᾗ στοιχειοῦσι.

[9]B: ὄφεων καὶ σκορπήον καὶ δρά-
 κοντος καὶ τὸν λοιπῶν παντῶν
 ἰοβίλον.
 C: ὄφεων σκορπίον καὶ δρακόντων
 καὶ λοιπὸν ἰοβόλον.
 D: δράκοντες σκορπίοι ὄφεις καὶ
 πάντα τὰ ἰοβόλα.
 E: ὄφεων καὶ σκορπίων καὶ δρακόντων καὶ τῶν λοιπῶν παντῶν
 ἰοβόλων.
 F: ὄφεις σκορπίοι δράκοντες καὶ
 τὰ λοιπὰ πάντα ἰοβόλα.

[10]BE: ἡ ε' ὥρα.

[11]BE: σαγλάτ.
 C: σαλάκ.
 D: omits.
 F: σαγδάγ.

[12]BE: ἐν αὐτῇ τῇ ὥρᾳ.
 C: τῇ αὐτῇ ὥρᾳ.

[13]BE: καί for ὅτε.
 C: τῇ αὐτῇ ὥρᾳ.
 F: omits αἰνεῖ and ὅτε.

[14]BE: add ἐν αὐτῇ τῇ ὥρᾳ.

[15]BE: πᾶν στοιχεῖον τετραπόδων
 λέοντος πάρδου ἄρκτου
 λύκου καὶ τῶν ὁμοίων.
 C: πᾶν στοιχίων τετράποδον
 λέοντες πάρδου λύκου
 καὶ λοιπῶν θηρίων.
 DF: πᾶν τετράποδον.

[16]BE: ἡ ἕκτη ὥρα.

[17]BE: τηεχμούλ.
 C: χακούλ.
 D: omits.
 F: χμούλ πημάλ.

[18]BE: ἐν αὐτῇ τῇ ὥρᾳ.
 C: τῇ αὐτῇ ὥρᾳ.
 F: omits.

[19]C: ἐνοῦσι.

[20]BCE: τὰ χερουβίμ τοῦ γένους
 τῶν (B: τόν).
 F: omits τά.

[21]F: ἀν[θρώπ]ῳ.

4   The 4th hour is called <u>slkn</u> in which all
    things made give thanks to God; in which
    <u>drkwnṭś</u>, <u>'wpwyś</u>, <u>śkwrpy'wy</u> [serpents, snakes,
    scorpions][a] and all poisonous creatures are
    charmed.[b]

5   The 5th hour is called <u>ś'lṭ</u> in which every
    living thing praises God; when every (spell
    concerning)[c] <u>ṭṭrpwn</u> [four-footed beasts][d] is
    conjured.

6   The 6th hour is called <u>ṭkmwl</u> (in) which the
    cherubim[e] importune God in behalf of human
    beings.

─────────────

a. I.e., δράκοντες, ὄφεις, and σκορπίοι. These are
obviously Greek words, and the other five MSS give the Greek
forms which are undoubtedly original. The Hebrew lettering
appears to be an affectation by the scribe of MS A.

b. The reading of BCEF is perhaps better: "in this hour
every spell concerning snakes and scorpions and serpents is
conjured."

c. Supplying στοιχεῖον, as found in BCE.

d. I.e., τετράπουν.

e. Note that the words cherubim and seraphim, of Hebrew
origin and written here with the Hebrew plural ending, are not
written in Hebrew characters, though many Greek words are. This
further weakens the view that the Hebrew words of MS A are transliterations from a Hebrew original.

7   Ὥρα ζ´[1] καλεῖται <u>ורוב</u>[2] ἐν ᾗ[3] αἰνοῦσιν[4] ἀγγέλων τάγματα[5] καὶ[6] παριστάμενα τῷ θεῷ.[7]

8   Ὥρα η´ καλεῖται <u>וירן</u>.[8]

9   Ὥρα θ´[9] καλεῖται <u>כטורונ</u>[10] ἤ χαπαυροῦν[11] ἐν ᾗ οὐδὲν τελεῖται.[12]

10 Ὥρα ι´[13] καλεῖται <u>ורוכונ</u>[14] ἤ <u>מוכומ</u>[15] ἐν ᾗ[16] ἑνοῦσιν[17] τὰ[18] ὕδατα[19] καὶ πνεῦμα θεοῦ καταβαῖνον[20] ἐπιπολάζει αὐτοῖς[21] καὶ ἁγιάζει[22] αὐτά. εἰ γὰρ μὴ[23] οὕτως[24] ἦν[25] ἔβλαπτον ἄν[26] οἱ πονηροὶ[27] δαίμονες ἀνθρώπους.[28]

---

[1] BE: Ἡ ζ´ ὥρα (B omits ὥρα).

[2] B: βερούκι.
C: βαρούκ.
D: omits name.
E: βερούκ.

[3] BE: ἐν αὐτῇ τῇ ὥρᾳ.
C: τῇ αὐτῇ ὥρᾳ.
F: omits ἐν ᾗ.

[4] B: αἰνοῦνται.

[5] BE: τὰ τάγματα τῶν ἀγγέλων.

[6] BCEF: omit καί.

[7] BCE: ἔμπροσθεν τοῦ θεοῦ.
F: ἥπνα ἱστάμενα τῷ θεῷ.

[8] BE: omit this entire hour.
C: βουράν.
D: omits name.
F: βηράν.

[9] BE: ἡ ἐννάτη (E: θ´) ὥρα.

[10] B: χαπβρόμ.
C: χαπβρούμ.
D: omits name.
E: χαπβρούη.
F: χατέρουν.

[11] D: χαπαυρούβ.
F: χαιπαρούκ.

[12] BCE: omit ἤ...τελεῖται.

[13] BE: Ἡ δεκάτη (E: ι´) ὥρα.

[14] BE: βουχοῦν.
C: βαχούμ.
D: omits name.
F: βρουχούν.

[15] BCDE: omit.
F: ἤ βουχούμ.

[16] BE: ἐν αὐτῇ.
C: τῇ αὐτῇ ὥρᾳ.

[17] BDEF: αἰνοῦσιν.
C: αἰνοῦνται.

[18] C: omits τά.

[19] BCE: add τὸν θεόν.

[20] C: καταβένον.
F: omits καταβαῖνον.

[21] BCE: ἐπιπολάζει ἐπάνω τῶν
         ὑδάτων.
F: ἐπιπολάζω αὐτῆς.

[22] F: ἡγιάζη.

[23] BE: εἰ μὴ γάρ.

[24] BCE: τοῦτο.
F: οὕτος.

[25] B: adds διὰ τὸν ὕδατον ὕδατος.
C: adds διὰ τοῦ ὕδατος.

[26] BE: ἄν ἔβλαπτον (B: ἔβλυττον).
F: omits ἄν.

[27] C: πονιροί.
E: omits πονηροί.

[28] BCE: δαίμονες τὸ γένος τῶν
         ἀνθρώπων.

7   The 7th hour is called <u>wrwk</u>, in which the
     ranks of angels which are standing by[a] praise
     God.

8   The 8th hour is called <u>wyrn</u>.[b]

9   The 9th hour is called <u>ktwrwn</u> or <u>chapauroun</u>,
     in which nothing is conjured.

10   The 10th hour is called <u>wrwkwn</u> or <u>mwkwm</u>, in
     which the waters (give) praise[c] and the spirit
     of God, descending, hovers over them and
     sanctifies them.[d] If it were not so the wicked
     demons would harm human beings.

---

     a.   Omitting καί. παριστάμενα modifies τάγματα not
ἀγγέλων. It is clear that the angelology presupposed here is
Jewish or Christian, and could not have originated with
Apollonius of Tyana, a pagan.

     b.   Note that the function of this hour and the part of
creation that offers praise in it are not given; what is
important in the Greek is the name of the hour, not its function.
Also note that B follows the error of E in omitting this entire
hour. Since B is the younger manuscript, it follows that it is
closely related to, and perhaps descended from, E.

     c.   Following the reading of BDEF.

     d.   Although all mention of Adam is missing, the biblical
flavor of the hours remains. It is unlikely that this passage,
with its allusions to the first chapter of Genesis, could have
been written by Apollonius of Tyana. See below pp. 138-39, 154.

ἐν ᾗ[1] ἐὰν ἄνθρωπος[2] נרונ ἄρῃ καὶ μίξει[3] μετὰ ἀγίου
ἐλαίου[4] πᾶν נושום[5] ἰαται[6] καὶ δαιμονόντας[7] καθαίρει[8]
καὶ δαίμονας ἀπελαύνει.[9]

11 Ὥρα ια·[10] καλεῖται שימירו ἢ שיאונ[11] ἐν ᾗ[12] εὐφραίνονται
οἱ ἐκλεκτοὶ[13] τοῦ θεοῦ.

12 Ὥρα ιβ·[14] καλεῖται אכליאו·[16] αἰνεῖ εὐπρόσδεκτοι αἱ
τῶν ἀνθρώπων εὐχαί.[17]

---

[1]BE: ἐν ταύτῃ τῇ ὥρᾳ.
C: σήμε ταύτῃ ὥρᾳ.
F: omits ἐν ᾗ.

[2]BE: εἰ ἄνθρωπος.
BCE: add καθαρός.

[3]BCE: ἄρῃ ὕδωρ καὶ μίξῃ (C: μίξι).
D: gives γέρων for נרונ (D[marg]:
νέρον).
F: λάβῃ ὕδωρ καὶ μίξῃ.

[4]C: μετ᾽ ἐλαίου.

[5]BF: νόσιμα.
DE: νόσημα.

[6]BE: ἰάσεται.
F: omits ἰαται.

[7]B: δέμονες.
C: δαιμονιόντας.
D: δαιμονοῦντας.
E: δαιμονῶντας.
F: δαιμονιῶντας.

[8]BE: καθαρίσει.
C: καθαρίζει.
F: ὑγιάζει.

[9]BCE: καὶ ἀπελάσει δαίμονας (B:
δέμονας).
F: omits.

[10]BE: ἡ ἐνδεκάτη (E: ια᾽) ὥρα.

[11]BE: καλεῖται σημβροῦ.
C: καλεῖτε σιμβροῦ.
D: καλεῖται (space) ἢ (space).
F: καλεῖται συμιροῦ ἢ σιοούρ.

[12]BE: ἐν αὐτῇ (E: adds τῇ) ὥρᾳ.
C: ἐν ταύτῃ τῇ ὥρᾳ.
F: ἐν οὖν καί.

[13]C: ἄγγελοι.

[14]BE: ἡ δωδεκάτη (E: ιβ᾽) ὥρα.

[15]B: καλλεῖται.

[16]BE: δακνειοῦν.
C: δαχλιοῦμ.
D: omits name.
F: ἀχλιοῦν.

[17]BE: ἐν αὐτῇ εὐπρόσδεκτοί εἰσιν
αἱ εὐχαὶ τῶν ἀνθρώπων παρὰ
(E: πρός) θεόν.
C: τῇ αὐτῇ ὥρᾳ εἰσιν εὐπρόσ-
δεκτος παρὰ τῷ θεῷ αἱ
προσευχαὶ τῶν ἀνθρώπων.
F: ἐν οὖν ᾗ εἰσιν εὐπρόσδεκτοι
ἐ τὸν οὐρανὸν εὐχαί.

In which (hour) if a man should take nrwn
[water]^a and mix (it) with holy oil, every
nwsyma [disease]^b is cured and the demon-
possessed^c are cleansed, and it drives away
demons.

11   The 11th hour is called ṣymyrw [today]^d or
      ṣy'wn [Zion]^e in which the elect of God^f rejoice.

12   The 12th hour is called 'kly'w; [in which]^g
      the prayers of human beings are acceptable.

---

   a. Note the use of the modern word νερόν for ὕδωρ, an
indication of the relatively late date of the Greek tradition.

   b. I.e., νόσημα.

   c. Following the reading of D.

   d. I.e., σήμερον.

   e. I.e., Σιών.

   f. "The elect of God" is another phrase which would be
unlikely to come from Apollonius of Tyana. The Syriac reads
"the righteous."

   g. Lit. "praises (verb)." αἰνεῖ should be emended to
ἐν ᾗ as in F, for which BCE always give the same variants as
they do here and which always follows the name of the hour in
MS A.

Ὀνομασίαι ὡρῶν νυκτερινῶν[1]

1 Ὥρα α΄.[2] καλεῖται[3] שוכרלרם[4] ἐν ᾗ οἱ δαίμονες αἰνοῦντες
τὸν θεὸν[5] οὔτε ἀδικοῦσιν οὔτε κολάζουσιν.[6]

2 Ὥρα β΄.[7] καλεῖται לרטטפשרא ἤ טטפשלרב[8] ἐν ᾗ[9] ὑμνοῦσιν[10]
οἱ ἰχθύες[11] τὸν θεὸν καὶ[12] τὸ τοῦ πυρὸς βάθος· ἐν
ᾗ ὀφείλει στοιχειοῦσθαι ἀποτελέσματα[13] εἰς δράκοντας
καὶ אורפיש[14] καὶ πῦρ.[15]

3 Ὥρα γ΄.[16] καλεῖται טכרב ἐν ᾗ[17] αἰνοῦσιν ὄφεις καὶ κύνες
καὶ πῦρ.[18]

---

[1] BE: περὶ τῶν ιβ΄ ὡρῶν τῆς
νυκτός.
C: περὶ τῶν ὀνομάτων τῶν ὁρῶν
τῆς νυκτός.
F: ὀνομασίαι ὡρῶν τῆς νυκτός.

[2] BE: Ἡ α΄ (B omits α΄) ὥρα τῆς
νυκτός.

[3] B: καλλεῖται.

[4] BE: σουχουλούμ.
C: δουχαλάμ.
D: omits name.

[5] BE: ἐν αὐτῇ αἰνοῦσιν οἱ δαίμονες τὸν θεὸν καὶ ἐν αὐτῇ.
C: ἐν ταύτῃ τῇ ὥρᾳ αἰνοῦσιν οἱ
δαίμονες τὸν θεὸν ταύτῃ τῇ
ὥρᾳ.
F: ἐν ᾗ οἱ δαίμονες τὸν θεόν.

[6] BCE: add μέχρις (E: μέχρι) ἂν
ἡ δέησις αὐτῶν τελειωθῇ
(C: πληρωθῇ).

[7] BE: ἡ δευτέρα (E: β΄) ὥρα τῆς
νυκτός.

[8] BE: καλεῖται βεπτεροῦλ.
C: καλεῖται δεπελοῦρ.
D: καλεῖται (space) ἤ (space).
F: καλεῖται ὁσπτερουλὴ ἤ βεπ-
τελοῦν.

[9] BE: ἐν αὐτῇ.
C: τῇ αὐτῇ ὥρᾳ.

[10] BCDEF: αἰνοῦσι.

[11] C: ἰχθύαις.

[12] B: adds πᾶν ὅ ἐστιν ἐν τοῖς
ὕδασι.
C: adds πᾶν εἴτε ἐν τοῖς ὕδασι.
E: adds πᾶν εἴ τί ἐστιν ἐν τοῖς
ὕδασιν.

[13] F: τοῦ πυρὸς βάθος· ἐν ᾗ ὁ θέλον
στοιχειῶσαι ἀποτελέσματι.

[14] DF: ὄφεις.

[15] BCE: omit τὸ τοῦ πυρός...καὶ πῦρ.

[16] B: ἡ τρίτη ὥρα τῆς νύκτα.
E: ἡ γ΄ ὥρα τῆς νυκτός.

[17] BE: καλεῖται ταχρὰν ἐν αὐτῇ τῇ ὥρᾳ.
C: καλεῖται ταραχαρὰν τῇ αὐτῇ
ὥρᾳ.
D: καλεῖται ταδρὰν ἐν ᾗ.
F: τυχράν (omits καλεῖται and
ἐν ᾗ.)

[18] BE: αἰνοῦσιν οἱ δράκοντες τὸν
θεὸν καὶ τὸ τοῦ πυρὸς βάθος
καὶ πάντα ὅσα εἰσὶν κατὰ
τῆς ἀνθρωπίνης φύσεως (E:
κατωτέρω ἃ ἡ ἀνθρωπίνη φύσις) νοῆσαι ἤ ἐξειπεῖν (B
adds παντῶς) οὐ δύναται. ἐν
αὐτῇ τῇ ὥρᾳ ὀφείλει ποιεῖν
στοιχειῶσιν ἀποτελεσμάτων
εἰς δράκοντάς τε καὶ ὄφεις
(E adds καὶ) περὶ πυρός.
C: αἰνοῦσιν οἱ δράκοντες τὸ θεὸν
καὶ τὰ τοῦ πυρὸς βάθος καὶ
πάντα ὅσα εἰσὶ κατώτερα ἡ
ἀνθρωπίνη φύσις εξειπῆν ἤ
νοῆσαι ἀδύνατον τῇ αὐτῇ ὥρᾳ
ὀφείλει ποιῆν ἀποτελεσμάτων
εἰς δράκοντας καὶ ὄφεις καὶ
πῦρ.

The Names of the Hours of the Night

1   The 1st hour is called s̀wkwlwm, in which the
     demons, (while) praising God, neither injure
     nor punish.[a]

2   The 2nd hour is called 'ws̀pṭrwl or ṭpṭlwn,
     in which the fish and the fiery deep[b] sing
     praise to God; in which (hour) one must charm
     talismans[c] against serpents and 'wpwys̀ [snakes][d]
     and fire.

3   The 3rd hour is called ṭkrn, in which snakes
     and dogs and fire give praise.[e]

_____

   a. The meaning seems to be that the demons neither injure
those on earth nor punish those in hell. The idea that the
demons have a role in punishing is not found in the Syriac.

   b. Lit. "the depth of fire." BCE add "and all that is
in the waters," in agreement with the Syriac.

   c. I.e., at this hour one must endow the talisman with
its power by means of a spell. Apollonius of Tyana was especially noted for making talismans. This meaning for ἀποτελέσματα,
though rare, has been conclusively demonstrated by Blum, *Eranos*
44 (1946) 317. See also J. Miller, "Zur Frage nach der Persönlichkeit des Apollonius von Tyana," *Philologus* 51 (1892) 581-84.

   d. I.e., ὄφεις, as in DF.

   e. E reads "in which the serpents and the fiery deep and
whatever is below, which human nature is unable to know or to
declare, praise God. In the same hour one ought to make magic
talismans against serpents and snakes and fire." Note the
parallel to the Syriac recension 2, 2:3.

4 Ὥρα δ'¹ καλεῖται אָנְגֵירִילַיִיר² ἐν ᾗ διέρχονται³ δαίμονες
   ἐν τοῖς μνήμασιν⁴ καὶ ὁ ἐρχόμενος ἐκεῖσε⁵ βλαβήσεται
   καὶ φόβον καὶ φρίκην ἐκ τῆς τῶν δαιμόνων λήψεται
   φαντασίας.⁶ ἐν ᾗ ὀφείλει ἐνεργεῖν⁷ ἐπί τε שְׁפַרָא :
   כֹּהְחְתָ καὶ παντὸς γοητικοῦ πράγματος.⁸

5 Ὥρα ε'⁹ καλεῖται¹⁰ בַּשְׁמַר¹¹ ἐν ᾗ αἰνοῦσιν τὰ ἄνω ὕδατα
   τὸν θεὸν τοῦ οὐρανοῦ.¹²

6 Ὥρα ϛ'¹³ καλεῖται שְׁרוּזִי¹⁴ ὅτε δέον ἡσυχάζειν¹⁵ καὶ ἀναπαῦσαι διότι ἔχει φόβον.¹⁶

---

¹BE: ἡ τετάρτη (E: δ') ὥρα τῆς
   νυκτός.

²B: ὐγχέλ.
 C: ἰαχήμ.
 D: omits name.
 E: ἀγχέλ.
 F: ἀϊαήλ ἢ χίλμ.

³BE: ἐν αὐτῇ τῇ ὥρᾳ διέρχονται
   οἱ.
 C: τῇ αὐτῇ ὥρᾳ διερχῶνται οἱ.
 F: adds οἱ.

⁴F: μνημείοις.

⁵B: καὶ εἰ περὶ οἷος ἄνθρωπος
   διέλθῃ ἐκεῖ.
 C: καὶ εἰ ἄνθρωπος διέλθῃ ἐκεῖ.
 E: καὶ οἷος ἄνθρωπος διέλθῃ
   ἐκεῖ.
 F: καὶ ὁ διερχόμενος ἐκεῖσε.

⁶BCE: λήψεται ἐκ τῆς τῶν
   δαιμόνων φαντασίας.
 F: τὸν δεμὸν for τῶν δαιμόνων.

⁷BE: ἡ δ' αὐτῇ (B adds τῇ) ὥρα
   ἐπιτελεῖ.
 C: εἰ δὲ αὐτῶν τῶν ἐνεργῶν.
 F: ἐνεργή.

⁸BE: ἐπί τε (23 cryptographs)
   καὶ εἰς πᾶν (13 cryptographs).
 C: ἐπί τε ἀγάπην καὶ ἔχθραν
   καὶ δεσμοῖς καὶ πᾶν ἐναν-
   τίων πρᾶγμα.
 D: omits Hebrew letters.
 F: ἐπὶ τῆς ἀγάπης καὶ ἔχθρας.

⁹BE: Ἡ πέμπτη (E: ε') ὥρα τῆς
   νυκτός.
 C: omits this entire hour.

¹⁰B: καλλεῖταν.

¹¹BE: κοσγάρ.
 D: omits name.
 F: καντάρ.

¹²BE: ἐν αὐτῇ τῇ ὥρᾳ αἰνοῦσιν τὰ
   ἐπάνω τοῦ οὐρανοῦ ὕδατα
   τὸν θεὸν καὶ τὸ ποιήματα
   αὐτοῦ.
 F: αἰνοῦσιν τὰ ὕδατα τὰ ὑπερ-
   άνω τοῦ οὐρανοῦ τὸν οὐραν-
   όν.

¹³BE: ἡ ϛ ὥρα τῆς νυκτός.
 C: ὥρα ε'.

¹⁴BCEF: ζερούς.
 D: omits name.

¹⁵BE: ἐν αὐτῇ τῇ ὥρᾳ δέον ἡσυ-
   άζειν.
 C: τῇ αὐτῇ ὥρᾳ δέον ἡσυγλάζην.
 F: δέον ἐστὶ ἡσυχᾶσαι.

¹⁶BCE: καὶ ἀναπαύεσθαι ἔχει γὰρ
   (F. Boll emends by adding
   οὐ) μικρὸν φόβον.
 F: καὶ ἀναπαῦσε ἔχει φόβον.

4   The 4th hour is called ''wyl'wyl, in which
     the demons go through the tombs, and whoever
     comes to that place will be harmed, and he
     will suffer fear and trembling from the
     appearance of the demons. In (this hour)[a]
     one ought to be engaged in 'rpś, khktrś,
     [love and hate][b] and every magical act.[c]

5   The 5th hour is called kśmr, in which the
     waters above praise the God of heaven.[d]

6   The 6th hour is called zrwś, when it is
     necessary to be quiet and rest, because
     it holds fear.[e]

---

a. Lit. "in which."

b. The Hebrew כ here is equivalent to the Greek καί.
See verse 2:8. The ר should probably be emended to ב, to agree
with CF ἀγάπης καὶ ἔχθρας.

c. This very difficult passage is different in all six
MSS. E offers no less than thirty-six cryptograms.

d. B and E probably preserve the better reading: "the
waters above heaven praise God," which also parallels the
Syriac.

e. It is unclear grammatically whether the hour holds
fear for man, or whether the man has fear of the hour, which
is midnight.

7 'Ὥρα ζ' καλεῖται מכלו[1] ἐν ᾗ[1] ἀναπαῦσαι[2] πάντα ζῷα ταῦτα.
   ἐάν τις ἄνθρωπος καθαρὸς ἁρπάσῃ[3] נרו[4] καὶ βάλλει[5]
   αὐτὸ ὁ[6] ἱερεὺς καὶ μίξει[7] μετ' ἐλαίου[8] καὶ ἁγιάσει[9]
   αὐτὸ καὶ ἀλλείψει[10] ἀπ' αὐτὸ[11] ἀσθενεῖ[12] ἀγρυπνοῦν-
   τα[13] παρευθὺ[14] τῆς νόσου[15] ἀπαλαγήσεται.[16]

8 'Ὥρα η'[17] καλεῖται דנר[18] ἐν ᾗ δὲ[19] ἀποτέλεσμαν στοιχει-
   οῦν[20] περὶ דנדרו : כאמפלו : כדורבטיאון[21] καὶ παν-
   τοίων φυτῶν.[22]

---

[1]BE: 'Η ἐβδόμη (E: ζ') ὥρα τῆς
   νυκτὸς καλεῖται μαχλοὺχ ἐν
   αὐτῇ τῇ ὥρᾳ.
C: "Ὥρα ζ' καλεῖται μαχλὸμ τῇ
   αὐτῇ ὥρᾳ.
D: omits name.
F: "Ὥρα ζ' μαχλοῦ ἐν ᾗ.

[2]B: ἀναπαυβοῦνται.
CEF: ἀναπαύονται.

[3]BCE: πάντα τὰ ζῷα καὶ οἱ ἄν-
   θρωποι ὑπνοῦσι ταύτῃ δὲ
   τῇ ὥρᾳ (C: τῇ αὐτῇ ὥρᾳ)
   ἐάν ἄνθρωπος ἁρπάσῃ (B:
   ἐάν ἁρπάσῃ ἄνθρωπος).
F: omits

[4]BCEF: ὕδωρ.
D: νέρον.

[5]BCE: λάβῃ.
F: βάλῃ.

[6]E: omits ὁ.

[7]CE: μίξῃ.
F: βάλῃ.

[8]BE: μετὰ ἁγίου ἐλαίου.
F: καὶ ἅγιον ἔλαιον.

[9]EF: ἁγιάσῃ.

[10]BCD: ἀλείψει.
EF: ἀλείψῃ (F adds ἀσθενῇ).

[11]D: ἄπαν τό.
BCE: omits.
F: ἀπ' αὐτοῦ and adds ἁγγιάζι
   αὐτόν.

[12]BE: ἀσθενοῦντα.
C: ἀσθενεῖν.
F: omits.

[13]B: ἀναγρυπνεῖ.
E: ἀναγρυπνῇ.
F: ἀγριπνοῦντι.

[14]BCF: παρευθύς.

[15]B: ὁ νόσος.

[16]DEF: ἀπαλλαγήσεται.

[17]BE: omit this entire hour.

[18]CF: ζάνβε.
D: omits name.

[19]C: ὀφείλει τῇ αὐτῇ ὥρᾳ.
D: δεῖ.
F: δέχου.

[20]C: ἀποτέλεσμα στοιχιῶται.

[21]C: δένδρον καὶ χοραφίων, ἀμ-
   πελώνων τε καὶ ἐλαιώνων.
DF: δένδρων καὶ ἀμπέλων καὶ
   δορατίων (F: χοραφίου).

[22]C: πάντων τῶν φυτῶν.
F: παντίον φητόν.

7   The 7th hour is called mklw, in which all
     these living things rest.[a] If any pure man
     should take nrwn [water][b] and the priest
     should take[c] it and mix (it) with oil and
     consecrate it and he anoints with it one
     (who is) wakeful with sickness, he will
     immediately be cured[d] of the disease.

8   The 8th hour is called dnw, in which one
     must[e] charm a talisman[f] for dndrwn, k'mplwn
     kdwrty'wn [trees and vineyards and staves][g]
     and all kinds of plants.

---

a. Reading with CEF, ἀναπαύονται.

b. I.e., νέρον.

c. Following the reading of BCE. A reads literally
"should cast."

d. Cp. Jas 5:14-15.

e. Following the reading of D. This is further indication
that D might not be influenced by A alone, since it preserves
the better reading not found in A.

f. Reading with C, ἀποτέλεσμα.

g. I.e., δένδρων, καὶ ἀμπέλων, καὶ δορατίων, as in DF.
Again, the Hebrew כ is the Greek καί. Note also that although
the Hebrew letters are read from right to left, the words themselves are read from left to right, a further indication that
these words have not been transcribed from a Hebrew original.

9 Ὥρα ϑ'[1] καλεῖται שׁפטנר.[2]

10 Ὥρα ι'[3] καλεῖται בלמו[4] ἐν ᾗ τελεῖται[5] οὐδέν.[6]

11 Ὥρα ια'[7] καλεῖται בלמו[8] ἐν ᾗ[9] ἀνοίγονται[10] αἱ πύλαι
    τοῦ οὐρανοῦ καὶ ἄνθρωπος ἐν κατανύξει εὐχόμενος[11]
    εὐήκοος γενήσεται.[12] ἐν ταῦτα[13] πέτονται[14] ταῖς
    πτέρυξιν σὺν ἤχῳ οἱ ἄγγελοι[15] καὶ[16] χερουβίμ
    καὶ[17] σεραφίμ καὶ ἔστιν χαρὰ ἐν[18] οὐρανῷ καὶ[19]
    γῇ· ἀνατέλλει[20] δὲ καὶ[21] ὁ[22] ἥλιος ἐξ εδέμ.[23]

---

[1]BE: Ἡ ἐννάτη (E: ϑ') ὥρα τῆς
νυκτός.

[2]BE: σοφγοῦ.
C: σοφιοῦ.
D: omits name.
F: σωφγοῦ.

[3]BE: ἡ δεκάτη (E: ι') ὥρα τῆς
νυκτός.
C: omits this hour.
James combines hours ϑ' and
ι', not seeing the superlinear
ὥρα ι'.

[4]B: χάλγου.
D: omits name.
EF: χάλτου.

[5]F: τελίος.

[6]BE: omit ἐν...οὐδέν.

[7]BE: ἡ ἑνδεκάτη (E: ια') ὥρα
τῆς νυκτός.
C: ὥρα ι'.

[8]BE: γάλγου.
C: σάλτου.
D: omits name.
F: γάλτου.

[9]BE: ἐν αὐτῇ.
C: τῇ αὐτῇ ὥρᾳ.

[10]C: ἀνοίγωνται.

[11]B: (after οὐρανοῦ) καὶ εὐπροσ-
δεχόμενος ἐν καθαρᾷ συνήδεισι
καὶ καρδίᾳ.
C: (after οὐρανοῦ) προσευχόμενος
ἐν καθαρᾷ καρδίᾳ καὶ συνηδήσει.

C: (after οὐρανοῦ) προσευχόμενος ἐν καθαρᾷ καρδίᾳ καὶ
συνηδήσει.
E: (after οὐρανοῦ) καὶ ὁ προσευχόμενος ἐν καθαρᾷ συνει-
δήσει καὶ καρδίᾳ.

[12]B: ἀκουστὸς γίνεται.
C: ἐπίκοος γίνεται.
E: εὐάκουστος γίνεται.

[13]BCE: ἐν αὐτῇ (C: ταύτῃ) ὥρᾳ.

[14]B: περὶ ἱπτάνεται.
C: περιήτταναι.
E: περιίπτανται.
F: πέτουνται.

[15]C: οἱ ἄγγελοι σὺν ἤχῳ.

[16]BCE: add τά.

[17]BCE: add τά.

[18]BCE: add τῷ.

[19]BCEF: add ἐν τῇ (F omits γῇ).

[20]C: ἀνατέλη.

[21]B: omits δὲ καί.

[22]B: omits ὁ.

[23]BCE: add ἐπὶ πᾶσαν τὴν γῆν.

9   The 9th hour is called šwpgw.[a]

10   The 10th hour is called kltw, in which
     nothing is conjured.[b]

11   The 11th hour is called gltw, in which
     the gates of heaven are opened and a man
     praying in contrition[c] will be readily heard.
     In this (hour) the angels and cherubim and
     seraphim fly with noisy wings[d] and (there) is
     joy in heaven and (on) earth; and the sun rises
     from Eden.[e]

---

a. Note that no information is given about this hour
except its name.

b. The same as in the 9th hour of the day (1:9).

c. This word, κατάνυξις, properly translated "slumber,"
or "stupor," in classical and Koine Greek, takes on the meaning
"compunction," and hence "contrition" in the early Byzantine
period. Compare the entries of Liddell and Scott with those of
Lampe and Sophocles.

d. Lit. "with wings with noise."

e. Lit. "Edem." Where the Syriac has "the paradise of
God," the Greek specifies Eden. Note that the reading of BCE
adds "over all the earth" which is closer to the Syriac than ADF.

12 Ὥρα ιβ΄[1] καλεῖται ‫עליש‬ ἤ ‫אלשיג‬[2] ἐν ᾗ[3] ἀναπαύονται[4]
    τὰ πύρινα τάγματα.[5] αὗται εἰσὶν αἱ ὀνομασίαι
    τῶν ὡρῶν[6] τῷ οὖν[7] καλῶς ταῦτα[8] νοήσαντι[9] οὐδὲν
    τῶν ὄντων[10] ἀποκρηβήσεται[11] ἀλλὰ πάντα[12] ὑποταγή-
    σονται.[13]

---

[1]BE: ἡ δωδεκάτη (E: ιβ΄) ὥρα.   [12]B: adds αὐτῶν.
   C: ὥρα ια΄ οὐ ὥρα ιβ΄.   CE: add αὐτῷ.

[2]B: εὔλσιν καλίν.   [13]C: ὑποταγήσεται.
   C: ἄσιν κελίν.   F: ὑποταγάσσονται.
   D: (space) ἤ (space).
   E: ἀλσιγκούλ.
   F: ἀλσὶν καὶ ἀλσίγγελος.

[3]BE: ἐν αὐτῇ τῇ ὥρᾳ.
   C: τῇ αὐτῇ ὥρᾳ.

[4]C: ἀναπαύωνται.

[5]BCE: τὰ τάγματα τοῦ οὐρανοῦ
       καὶ τὰ πύρινα τάγματα
       (C: πνεύματα).

[6]B: adds ὧν ἐπίησεν ὁ θεὸς ἐν
   ταῖς ζ΄ ἡμέραις καὶ ταῦτα
   ἔλαβον παρὰ θεὸν καὶ ἐδήλωσά σοι ὡς καθῶς καὶ ἐγνώρισα ταύτας ἔμαθα καὶ ἔλαβον
   παρὰ θεοῦ καὶ γνωρίσω καὶ
   ἐδήλωσα.
   C: adds ἃς ἐποίησεν τὰς ζ΄
   ἡμέρας καὶ ταῦτα ἔλαβον
   παρὰ θεοῦ καὶ ἐδήλωσά σοι
   ὡς καθῶς καὶ ἡγνώρησα καὶ
   ἔμαθον καὶ ἰδοὺ παρεδήλωσά
   σοι ἄπαντα.
   E: adds ὧν ἐποίησεν ὁ θεὸς ἐν
   ταῖς ζ΄ ἡμέραις· ταύτας
   ἔμαθον καὶ ἔλαβον παρὰ θεοῦ
   καὶ ἐγνώρισα καὶ ἐδήλωσά σοι.

[7]C: τούτ΄ οὖν.

[8]E: omits ταῦτα.

[9]B: τόριτι ἄλο νόησις τῇ.
   C: νοήσαντες.

[10]F: ὀνόντον.

[11]B: οὐκ ἀποκριθήσοντε τὸν ὡρῶν ὄντων οὐδέν.
    C: οὐκ ἀποκριβείσεταί τι τῶν ὄντων.
    DF: ἀποκρυβήσεται.
    E: οὐκ ἀποκρυβήσεται τῶν ὄντων οὐδέν.

12   The 12th hour is called '1ṡy, or '1ṡyn,
      in which the fiery ranks rest. These are
      the names of the hours;[a] therefore, to him
      who has learned them well nothing of what
      exists will be hidden, but all things will
      be made subject (to him).[b]

---

a. The biblical creation motif slips into the Greek text
time and again, as witnessed here by the variants BCE which
speak of the seven days of creation.

b. The importance of the names of the hours to magical
interests is nowhere made as clear as here, where the promise
is given that knowing the names will render all things subject
to the knower.

Historiarum Compendium 1:17-18[a]

"Ότι 'Αδὰμ τῷ ἑξακοσιοστῷ ἔτει μετανοήσας ἔγνω
δι' ἀποκαλύψεως τὰ περὶ τῶν 'Εγρηγόρων καὶ τοῦ κατα-
κλυσμοῦ, καὶ τὰ περὶ μετανοίας καὶ τῆς θείας σαρκώσεως,
καὶ περὶ τῶν καθ' ἑκάστην ὥραν ἡμερινὴν καὶ νυκτερινὴν
ἀναπεμπομένων εὐχῶν τῷ θεῷ ἀπὸ πάντων τῶν κτισμάτων
δι' Οὐριὴλ τοῦ ἐπὶ τῆς μετανοίας ἀρχαγγέλου, οὕτως·
"Ωρᾳ πρώτῃ ἡμερινῇ πρώτη εὐχὴ ἐπιτελεῖται ἐν τῷ οὐρανῷ,
δευτέρᾳ εὐχὴ ἀγγέλων, τρίτῃ εὐχὴ πτηνῶν, τετάρτῃ εὐχὴ
κτηνῶν, πέμπτῃ εὐχὴ θηρίων, ἕκτῃ ἀγγέλων παράστασις
καὶ διάκρισις πάσης κτίσεως, ἑβδόμῃ ἀγγέλων εἴσοδος
πρὸς θεὸν καὶ ἔξοδος ἀγγέλων, ὀγδόῃ αἴνεσις καὶ θυσίαι
ἀγγέλων, ἐννάτῃ δέησις καὶ λατρεία ἀνθρώπου, δεκάτῃ
ἐπισκοπαὶ ὑδάτων καὶ δεήσεις οὐρανίων καὶ ἐπιγείων,
ἑνδεκάτῃ ἀνθομολόγησις καὶ ἀγαλλίασις πάντων, δωδεκάτῃ
ἔντευξις ἀνθρώπων εἰς εὐδοκίας.

---

a.   Text from Bekker, *George Cedrenus*, vol. 1, pp. 17-8.

From the *Compendium* of George Cedrenus

Adam, in the six hundredth year,[a] having repented,
learned by revelation the things concerning the
Watchers and the Flood, and about repentance and the
divine Incarnation, and about the prayers that are
sent up to God by all creatures at each hour of the
day and night, with the help of Uriel, the archangel
over repentance. Thus, in the first hour of the
day the first prayer is completed in heaven; in the
second the prayer of angels; in the third the prayer
of winged things; in the fourth the prayer of domestic
animals; in the fifth the prayer of wild beasts; in
the sixth the review of the angels and the inspection
of all creation; in the seventh the entrance of the
angels to God and the exit of the angels; in the
eighth the praise and sacrifices of the angels; in
the ninth the petition and worship of men;[b] in the
tenth the visitations of the waters and the petition
of the heavenly and earthly (beings); in the eleventh
the thanksgiving and rejoicing of all (things); in
the twelfth the entreaty of human beings for favor.

---

a. Compare this with the Apocalypse of Adam, plate 64,
lines 2-4: "The revelation which Adam taught his son Seth
in the seven hundredth year."

b. Lit. "of a man."

A cursory study of the apparatus shows that D is a copy of
A. For this reason the importance of D as an independent witness is in serious doubt. Some passages in D, however, offer
readings not only different from, but even superior to those of
A.[15] Granted, the usual practice of D is to leave a blank space
corresponding to the Hebrew letters of A, but several times D
supplies the Greek word which A transliterates.[16] The most
interesting of these instances is at 2:3 where D reads ταδράν,
where A reads טכרנ. If the scribe of D could read the Hebrew
letters, why did he not render them as ταχράν, as do B and E?
If the scribe could not read the Hebrew letters, how did he know
the correct Greek word behind several other passages (see note
16 above)? The possibility must at least be left open that,
while D is a copy of A, it may have been compared against a
third manuscript. Nevertheless, this possibility should not be
given too much weight, since the "better" readings of D are also
the obvious emendations for those passages where A is corrupt,
and since the rendering of טכרנ by ταδράν may merely be a
mistake.

Manuscript F is also very close to A, though not, like D,
a direct copy. It is the most corrupt of the six manuscripts
and contains frequent spelling and tense errors. Although its
readings are generally inferior to those of A, they occasionally
shed some light on a difficult passage, as at 2:4 where F agrees
with C against ABDE. The occasional variant DF strengthens the
possibility that D, though a copy of A, was checked against a
third manuscript.

It seems relatively certain that the Hebrew letters found
in A are merely the device of a Greek scribe and form no link
between A and a hypothetical Hebrew original.[17] This is also
the conclusion of A. Delatte, who provides a table of Greek
letters for both the Hebrew letters and the magical symbols
found in this manuscript.[18] The names of the hours written in
Hebrew letters are similar to the names of the Stundengötter,
which are known from other Greek magical texts.[19] In addition
to the names of the hours, the scribe of A has also written an
occasional word of the Greek text in Hebrew letters.

The relationship between manuscripts B and E seems clear.
B is the younger of these two closely related documents.[20] C is

independent of either group ADF or BE. The most frequent group-
ing of the variants is ADF, BE, C, and C often stands in contrast to the other five manuscripts,[21] usually giving a different name to each hour than BE.[22] Nevertheless, C stands closer
to BE than to ADF, and the reading BCE against ADF is not
uncommon.[23] More often C shares a similar, though not identical,
reading with BE against ADF, as in the long addition at 2:8, or
the shorter one at 1:5.

Finally, it may be said that BCE are usually, though not
always, closer to the readings of the Syriac, especially of
Syriac recension 2. This is evident, for example, in the additions to ADF made by BCE at 2:2 and 2:3, or in numerous small
examples as in the reading "ὑπὲρ τοῦ γένους τῶν ἀνθρώπων" at
1:6.[24]

These six Greek manuscripts are distinctly concerned with
magic. This is evident from the emphasis placed on the names
of each hour and the connection of a given hour with an occult
operation appropriate to it alone. In the closing lines of the
document, the reader is assured that by knowing the names of
the hours "nothing of what exists will be hidden, but all things
will be made subject (to him)." The fourth hour of the night is
identified as the hour in which one ought to be engaged in
"every magical act." Moreover, the specific operations which
concern each hour in the Greek text are the preparation of
talismans against certain dangers or in protection of crops and
domestic animals.

The major problem in translating these six manuscripts
involves the terms στοιχεῖον and ἀποτελεῖν and their cognates.[25]
To render these terms by their respective classical meanings,
"element" and "to complete," provides an unsatisfactory translation, and the passages have baffled several critics. The entry
of G. W. Lampe apropos of these passages reads "ἀποτέλεσμα: ...
7. sens. dub., plu.? *created objects* στοιχειοῦσθαι α. εἰς δρά-
κοντος Apoc. Adam 2 (p. 142)."[26] Lampe also suggests that in a
magical text στοιχειόω should be rendered "transform," but in
support of this he offers only a reference to this passage.[27]
The assumption that these terms ought to be translated by their
classical equivalents is incorrect; the idiom involved here is
not classical, but Byzantine.

In an excellent article based in part on passages from our text, C. Blum has shown that the key to understanding στοιχεῖον and ἀποτελεῖν lies in the vocabulary of late Byzantine magic, particularly in the Byzantine traditions concerning Apollonius of Tyana.

> The Apollonius of Tyana who appears in Byzantine, Syrian and Arab folklore devotes himself chiefly to one occupation, viz. the producing of talismans against serpents, vermin, wild beasts, human enemies, floods and the like. The scene is Contantinople or Antioch. In the older Greek sources his talismans are called (ἀπο) τελέσματα, the verb being (ἀπο) τελεῖν. In the later chronicles στοιχειοῦν and στοιχειοῦσθαι, and στοιχεῖον, are used along with the earlier terms.[28]

Blum notes that στοιχειοῦσθαι replaces an earlier term (τελεῖν) in about the tenth or eleventh century, with the period of George Cedrenus the likely time of transition.

> The case is very clearly stated, when we come to the Palladium of Troy. Malalas speaks of ... τὸ Παλλάδιον ..., ὃ ἔλεγον εἶναι τετελεσμένον εἰς νίκην, φυλάττοντα τὴν πόλιν ἔνθα ἀπόκειται ἀπαράληπτον (p. 109, I). On the other hand, Cedrenus I p. 229, quoted above, says τετελεσμένον ... ἤτοι ... ἐστοιχειωμένον. It seems as if the chronicler had thought it advisable to explain τετελεσμένον by a more modern expression.[29]

After examining several passages from other writings, Blum concludes:

> All the material available indicates that στοιχειοῦσθαι and στοιχεῖον in the sense here suggested are a purely Byzantine idiom. The belief in talismans is universal, but from a lexicologic point of view we have nothing in the ancient literature to link up with. We have stated already, in a preliminary fashion, that our terms tended to supersede τελεῖν and its derivates, and this is abundantly brought out by a comparison of our sources with parallels dating from before "the dark centuries" of the Eastern Empire.[30]

Significantly, all of the witnesses to this magical meaning for στοιχεῖον are dated from the tenth century or later.[31]

Blum's rendering of ἀποτέλεσμα as "talisman" is widely supported.[32] Moreover, English etymologists trace the derivation of the word "talisman", which entered the language at about the seventeenth century, to the late Greek (ἀπο) τέλεσμα.[33] In view, therefore, of the marked emphasis on magic and the late

date suggested by the vocabulary, there can be little doubt that
the hours of the day and night as found in the Greek manuscripts
represent, as M. R. James observed in 1893,[34] a work of Byzantine
occultism.

CHAPTER V
LITERARY AND HISTORICAL QUESTIONS

Original Language

Three languages have been proposed as the language in which the Testament of Adam was originally composed. These are Hebrew, Greek and Syriac. Although the testament also exists in Arabic, Karshuni, Ethiopic, Old Georgian and Armenian, these may be excluded as candidates for the original language because of the comparatively late dates of their respective literary traditions.[1] A. Dillmann, E. Bratke and S. Grebaut have all dated the composition of the Arabic Book of the Rolls, in which the Testament of Adam is found, to the middle of the eighth century A.D.[2] And although there are, according to A. Graf,[3] Arabic manuscripts in which the Testament of Adam is found as an independent work separate from the Book of the Rolls, it is very unlikely that any Arabic manuscripts of the testament could have existed before the seventh century A.D., by which time it was already circulating in Syriac.[4] Beyond this, as G. Reinink has shown, the Arabic agrees consistently with Syriac recension 3, and not only repeats its expansions and errors relative to Syriac recension 1,[5] but reinterprets and expands its readings even further.[6] In addition, the Testament of Adam in the Arabic version is foreign to its context, and comes after the formula which is used in the rest of the composition to mark the end of a patriarch's words.[7] Finally, it must be noted that the Testament of Adam is always clearly labelled by name within the Book of the Rolls,[8] a fact which indicates a source pre-dating the composition of that document.[9]

As in the case of the Arabic, the Ethiopic, Karshuni, Old Georgian and Armenian versions cannot represent the original language of the Testament of Adam, since all of these languages developed at too late a date to be considered ahead of the Syriac. Moreover, it has been firmly established that

the Ethiopic is a direct translation of the Arabic.[10] The Old
Georgian version is also clearly a translation, although it is
not clear whether from Syriac or from Arabic. Z. Avalachvili
believes the source to be Syriac, since the Old Georgian
contains none of the pseudo-Clementine material found in the
Arabic and its dependent traditions.[11] If Avalachvili is
right, and it is by no means certain that he is, it may indicate that the Testament of Adam and the Cave of Treasures had
been joined together in Syriac before they were translated
into Arabic, and that the pseudo-Clementine attribution was
added to the Arabic version, from which it passed to the
Ethiopic. Either way, one thing is clear: Old Georgian cannot be the original language of the Testament of Adam.

    In comparing the Syriac and Arabic traditions, the Arabic
may be dismissed as a candidate for original language only
because the Syriac evidence pre-dates the rise of Arabic
literature by approximately two hundred years. Some have held
that in comparison to the Greek tradition, the Syriac might
similarly be dismissed. However, in comparing the Greek and
Syriac witnesses to the Testament of Adam we find that the
Syriac evidence is much earlier than the Greek.[12] It is true
that Greek manuscripts dated before the Christian era must
undoubtedly have priority over any Syriac manuscripts, but
the projection of this *a priori* past the first century A.D.
and the beginnings of the Syriac literary tradition represents
a methodological error of which several critics have been
guilty. When the Greek evidence in question all dates after
the tenth century A.D., as in the case of the Testament of
Adam, the operation of such a bias in favor of the Greek is
indefensible. Since the origins of the Testament of Adam date
from a period when both Greek and Syriac were widely spoken,
critical scholars should allow no *a priori* assumptions favor-
ing the originality of either language to prejudice their
investigation.

    Of the three languages mentioned above as possiblities,
Hebrew is least likely to be the original. The case for a
Hebrew original rests solely on the Hebrew characters from
Paris Greek manuscript 2419 (manuscript A). There are at
least four reasons why these Hebrew characters cannot be

transcriptions from a Hebrew original. First, though the
letters are Hebrew, the words (where decipherable) are
Greek.[13]   Second, though the Hebrew letters read from right
to left, the words in which they appear read from left to
right.[14]   Third, the Hebrew letters are found in only one of
the fourteen Greek and Syriac manuscripts. Fourth, those
words most likely to be derived from a Hebrew original, e.g.
the loan words cherubim and seraphim, are not written in
Hebrew letters but in Greek.[15]   In view of these facts, further
pursuit of a possible Hebrew original based on the Hebrew letters of Greek manuscript A would seem unnecessary. There is
no connection between the Hebrew names of manuscript A and
the Arabic names found in one Arabic manuscript noted by
Renan.[16]

     The remaining candidates for the original language of the
testament are Greek and Syriac. Since some have held that
part of the testament was composed in Greek and part in Syriac,
the question of original language is tied to a degree to the
question of literary unity. For this reason the evidence per-
taining to each part of the testament (Horarium, Prophecy and
Hierarchy), must be examined separately.

The Horarium

     It has been forcefully asserted by some critics that the
Horarium from the Testament of Adam comes from a Greek original witnessed by the citations of Syncellus and Cedrenus
and by the six magical manuscripts edited above. Although he
had never seen them, C. Bezold assumed that these Greek manuscripts represent a Greek original of the Horarium.[17]   Bezold's
assertion was accepted without further investigation by I.
Goldziher and others.[18]   However, the most eloquent proponent
of Greek priority was F. Nau, who in 1907 published an edition
of the four Greek manuscripts known to him.[19]   Nau was con-
vinced that the Horarium from the Testament of Adam was originally written in Greek by none other than Apollonius of
Tyana, and that the Prophecy was a later addition to the Syriac
version taken from the Syriac Cave of Treasures.[20]

     Nau pointed out that in several of the Greek manuscripts
the larger work which contains the Horarium, the *Apotelesmata*,

is attributed to Apollonius, and that the *Apotelesmata* is
exactly the sort of work one would expect Apollonius to have
written. Nau spends several pages demonstrating that the work
is consistent with the character of Apollonius of Tyana as it
is known from the ancient sources. He also accepts M. R.
James' argument for a Latin version of the Testament of Adam
and argues that this Latin version proves the antiquity of the
Horarium, since the author who quotes it, Nicetas of Remesiana, died about A.D. 414. Nau believed that the antiquity of
the Horarium, as evidenced by the proposed Latin version,
supported its attribution to Apollonius. Nau finally concluded:

> Unde neque gnosticus neque christianus est, sed
> promanat ex opere magico Apollonio Tyanensis
> adscripto. Sub patrocinio patris nostri Adam
> positum fuit ut servaretur ab igne cui dedita
> erant magiae opera, et etiam quia maxime patrem
> nostrum Adam decebat nomina omnibus entibus
> ponere. Unde *Testamentum Adam* erutum est partim
> e *spelunca Thesaurorum* et partim e *libro Apoteles-
> matum* Apollonii.[21]

There are several insurmountable difficulties with Nau's
view. First, that Apollonius of Tyana was *likely* to have
written such a document, hardly proves that he actually *did*
write it. Compatibility between the contents of a document
and the character of its supposed author might just as easily
prove the skill of its forger as the authenticity of its
attribution. Moreover, the *Apotelesmata* is not really as
compatible with the figure of Apollonius as Nau claimed. Not
all of the Greek manuscripts are attributed to Apollonius, and
in one, manuscript C, the Horarium is not found in connection
with the *Apotelesmata* at all. Even if one allows an *intended*
connection between the work and Apollonius, the *Apotelesmata*
can scarcely have been the product of a pagan author, since
chapter two begins: "He who is about to be born of a virgin
in Bethlehem will be a great teacher and will save the human
race, and will destroy the temples of idols."[22] The Greek
Horarium itself refers to cherubim (1:6), ranks of angels
(1:7), the spirit of God hovering over the waters (1:10),
anointing the sick with holy oil (1:10, 2:7), the elect of
God (1:11), the waters above (2:5), seraphim, the sun rising

from Eden (2:11) and, in manuscripts B, C and E, the seven
days of creation (2:12). These are hardly concepts consistent
with pagan authorship.

Finally, the manuscript evidence attributing the Horarium
to Apollonius of Tyana is not earlier than the fifteenth
century A.D. Nau's appeal to the possible existence of the
Horarium in Latin in the fourth century actually vitiates his
case, since, if James' conjecture be accepted at all, it
clearly establishes that such a work was known in that time
and place as the Testament of Adam and not as a work bearing
any connection with Apollonius of Tyana or with the *Apotelesmata* attributed to him. It is apparent that the Horarium could
could not in its present form have been written by Apollonius
of Tyana. It remains to be seen, however, whether the Horarium may not still have been composed in the Greek language,
albeit by a Jewish or Christian author.

The evidence against Greek as the original language of
the Horarium is impressive. First of all, the accounts of the
Horarium given by Syncellus and Cedrenus cannot be treated as
witnesses to a Greek original due to their extremely abbreviated nature and the propensity of these authors for collecting
scraps of tradition from a wide variety of sources and pasting
them together indiscriminately. While it is clear that Syncellus and Cedrenus are working from sources, there is no
evidence to indicate what sort of sources these may have been
or in what languages they may have been originally composed.
In short, the brief notes of Syncellus and Cedrenus represent
synopses of traditions known to them, taken from sources about
which we can only speculate.

Unlike the Greek, the Syriac assigns the hours of the
day and night to that entity most logically associated with
it. Thus, the order of events in the Syriac Horarium reflects
the natural order of the days' activities: doves coo in the
early evening; there is fear at midnight and dew in the morning; morning prayers and the crowing of the roosters are followed by the rising of the sun and the beginning of worship
services with the burning of incense.

Finally, the greatest objection to the priority of the
present Greek version is its agreement with Syriac recension 3,

the latest and most corrupt of the Syriac recensions; the
Greek preserves several of the expansions and errors of that
recension.[23] The agreement of the Greek with Syriac recension
3 against Syriac recension 1 can be demonstrated at several
points. Both mention dragons at 2:2, and both use letters
as ordinal numbers instead of writing them out as words.[24]
Both begin with the hours of the day rather than the hours of
the night and reflect the Roman rather than the Jewish reckoning. The Greek repeats an error that originates in the trans-
mission of the Syriac text. Syriac text E mistakenly reads
ܚܝ̈ܘܬܐ (beasts) for ܚܝ̈ܠܘܬܐ (powers) at 2:7; the Greek reading
is ζῷα (animals).

It is therefore likely that the present Greek text
depends upon the Syriac text. But may not the Syriac ultimately be derived from a different Greek *Urtext*? This seems
unlikely for several reasons. First of all, there are in the
Syriac text neither transliterations from Greek nor Greek loan
words which were not already part of the Syriac language (e.g.
ܐܓܝܢ and ܐܟܣܢܝܐ). Also, the syntax and grammar is entirely
Syriac. There are no examples of uncharacteristic construc-
tions which could be explained on the basis of translation
from a Greek original. Moreover, the variants found in the
several Syriac manuscripts are all internal Syriac variants;
that is, they can all be explained in terms of mistaking one
Syriac word for another, and could only occur in a Syriac
context. No variants suggest a misunderstood or mistranslated
Greek word. At 1:4 manuscript F reads ܪܘܚܢܝܐ (of the spiritual beings) which is an error for ܪܚܫܐ (of creeping things).
At 2:2, recension 3 reads ܢܘܢܐ (of the fish) where recension
1 reads ܝܘܢܐ (of the doves), but this error might also
involve ܢܘܪܐ (of fire) which is found in the same line. At
2:4 manuscripts F and H read ܒܚܝܠܐ (with the force) instead of
ܒܩܠܐ (with the sound). At 2:5 manuscript E reads ܓܝܓܠܐ (of
wheels) instead of ܓܠܠܐ (of waves). At 2:6 manuscript H
reads ܒܥܘܬܐ (petition), and F and G read ܥܩܒܬܐ (investigation), instead of ܪܘܟܒܐ (composition).

A. M. Denis implies that a "Jewish" original stands
behind both the Greek and Syriac versions of the Horarium.[25]
However, he does not specify the language of this Jewish

original, nor does he entertain the possibility that the best
candidate for such an original might be the Syriac itself.
Indeed, a Jewish original behind the Horarium must look so
much like the present Syriac text that the idea of an earlier
version in a different language is an unnecessary elaboration
of the hypothesis. If there is a "Jewish" original to the
Horarium, it may very well be found by scraping away the few
possibly Christian accretions from the present Syriac text.

In summary, it is clear that Apollonius of Tyana was not
the author of the Horarium. It was written by an anonymous
Christian or Jew, as is indicated by the strong biblical element in the narrative. The accounts of Syncellus and Cedrenus
do not represent a Greek original of the Horarium, and do not
support the readings or the priority of the six magical manuscripts. The Syriac manuscript evidence is far older than the
Greek. The magical elements of the Greek manuscripts are best
understood as material added to the Greek text rather than
deleted from the Syriac. The present Greek uses late vocabulary that dates from the tenth century A.D.,[26] and, moreover,
it agrees with the latest and least trustworthy of the Syriac
recensions. The Syriac, which is clearly prior to the extant
Greek text, does not appear from an examination of the internal evidence to be based on a Greek *Urtext*. All of this makes
it improbable in the extreme that Greek is the original language of the Horarium. Further, there is no reason to postu-
late a common source in a third language to explain the
relationship of the Greek and Syriac traditions relative to
the Horarium. Therefore, we must conclude with M. R. James,
J. B. Frey and G. J. Reinink that the original language of the
Horarium is Syriac.

The Prophecy

Even those critics who have insisted most forcefully on a
Greek original for the Horarium have not doubted the Syriac
origin of the Prophecy of Adam to Seth.[27] This is due in part
to an assumed connection between the Prophecy and the Syriac
Cave of Treasures. However, this assumption is correct only
insofar as it implies that both documents make use of similar
traditions; there is little evidence that one is dependent

literarily upon the other, or that the Prophecy was ever a
part of the Cave of Treasures.[28] Neither is there any manuscript evidence that the Prophecy was ever found in Greek.
It is found in the Arabic, Karshuni, and Ethiopic Book of the
Rolls, and in the Old Georgian Cave of Treasures. But, as in
the case of the Horarium, all of these literary traditions are
too late to be the original language of the Prophecy. This
leaves Syriac as the major possibility.

Some strong internal evidence for the originality of the
Syriac is the several striking paronomasiae found in the
Prophecy. The most notable of these is at 3:3, "Because you
listened to the words of the serpent (ܚܘܝܐ) you will become
food for the serpent." In this sentence ܚܘܝܐ is used the
first time with the meaning of "serpent," and the second time
with the meaning of "worm."[29] The passage is even more
striking in recension 2, where it reads: "Because you listened to the counsel of Eve (ܚܘܐ) you shall be (ܗܘܐ) food for
the serpent (ܚܘܝܐ)." The reading of recension 2 is also
superior to that of recension 1 in that it emphasizes the
assonance between ܚܘܐ, ܗܘܐ and ܚܘܝܐ.[30]

Another paronomasia found most notably at 3:5, reads:
"You have heard, my son Seth," but could also be translated
"I heard in the beginning." A check of the variants at this
point and others where the same words appear reveals that they
have even caused some confusion among the Syriac scribes.[31]
Also, at 3:2 we find the words: "and the maggot and the worm
will devour your body," where the word "maggot" (ܪܩܩܐ) can
also mean "a period of time."

The verse added to the end of the Prophecy in Syriac
recension 3 is taken from the writings of Ephraem Syrus, and
there can be little doubt as to its Syriac origin, although
this does not necessarily reflect on the rest of the Prophecy.
The combined evidence of the paronomasiae in the Syriac text,
the late dates of all versions but the Syriac, and the additions to Syriac recension 3 from the writings of Ephraem Syrus,
indicate a Syriac original for the Prophecy.

The Hierarchy

There is little doubt concerning the Syriac origin of the
Hierarchy, for it is extant in only one Syriac manuscript

(MS C), and there is no indication, either internal or external that it ever existed in another language. Moreover, the
quotation from Zechariah 1:8 found in verse 7 of the Hierarchy
follows the reading of the Peshiṭta version of the Old Testament, rather than the Septuagint.[32]

The possibility of a Greek original for the Hierarchy is
implied by an often assumed connection with the similar angelology in the "Celestial Hierarchy" of pseudo-Dionysius the
Areopagite (c. A.D. 500). Most critics have accepted the
suggestion of E. Renan that the former is dependent on the
latter.[33] However, the similarity between these two texts
has been greatly exaggerated, and any claim of literary
dependence between the two is inadvisable.[34] However, the
Hierarchy from the Testament of Adam is very similar to the
angelology from the Book of the Bee, by Solomon of Basra
(c. A.D. 1222).[35] It is, of course, possible that both go
back ultimately to the angelology of pseudo-Dionysius, but
this is highly unlikely since a third similar angelology[36] is
found in the opening lines of the Syriac Cave of Treasures,
which A. Götze has dated between the second and fourth
centuries.[37] This would indicate that pseudo-Dionysius may
have received the initial inspiration for his ranks of angels
from the Syriac tradition rather than vice versa, especially
since Götze has documented at least one other passage in which
pseudo-Dionysius is dependent upon the Syriac Cave of Treasures.[38]

But as the Hierarchy is not dependent upon the Celestial
Hierarchy of pseudo-Dionysius, neither is it dependent on the
angelology from the Book of the Bee. Rather there are several
reasons why the opposite seems to be the case. First, Solomon
of Basra was, like Cedrenus and Syncellus, a collector of
traditions more than their author. This is evident from the
end of the passage in question where Solomon actually enters
into debate with his source(s), and where he employs the formula "Some say . . . others say . . . ."[39] Second, the Hierarchy
is shorter than the angelology from the Book of the Bee and
manifests none of the philosophical concerns of the latter.
For example, the rather anthropomorphic angelic beings of the
Hierarchy have been transformed in the Book of the Bee into

mystical types of "motion" and other abstractions. Third,
the Old Testament references and Jewish elements of the Hierarchy have been deleted from the angelology in the Book of the
Bee.[40]

From all of the above, it is safe to conclude that the
Hierarchy from the Testament of Adam represents an independent
tradition which goes back in Syriac literature at least to the
origins of the Cave of Treasures in the second or third century, and probably to the New Testament and Jewish apocalyptic
literature.

Literary Unity

It is necessary to distinguish carefully the question of
literary unity from the question of an author's sources. The
question of possible sources will be taken up below. The
issue now to be discussed is this: Did the final redactor
intend that the Horarium, Prophecy and Hierarchy be read
together as a single document?

In the first critical treatment of the Testament of Adam
in modern times, E. Renan concluded that the testament was not
a unified document, but that it was a collection of random
fragments from a larger work.[41] Renan's conclusion was influenced by his reliance upon Syriac manuscript C, which is the
only Syriac manuscript to set the different sections of the
testament apart with the scribal interjections: "By our same
first father, our father Adam" (between the Horarium and
Prophecy), and "Also from the testament of our father Adam"
(between the Prophecy and Hierarhcy). Renan failed to note
the significance of the final interjection at the end of the
Hierarchy which reads: "In the strength of our Lord's help,
the end of the writing, the Testament of our father Adam,"
which would seem to attribute a unity to the preceding sections. Since Renan knew only manuscripts C and D, his conclusion that the testament was a collection of fragments is perhaps understandable. Unfortunately, he was followed in his
conclusion by most subsequent critics who continued to call
the Testament of Adam a collection of fragments even after
more manuscript evidence had been found.[42] When F. Nau and
others began insisting that the Horarium, unlike the Prophecy

and Hierarchy, was originally composed in Greek, the "fragmentary" hypothesis became even more firmly entrenched.

The Horarium and Prophecy

Although the "fragmentary" hypothesis has been generally
accepted, there is quite a bit of evidence to indicate that
the Horarium and the Prophecy constitute a single document.
First, all the versions except the Greek, which is very late,
contain both. Second, of the four Syriac manuscripts which
do not contain both the Horarium and the Prophecy, manuscripts
E and H explicitly state that their accounts are excerpts, and
manuscript D is extremely likely to have omitted the Horarium
purposely.[43] Third, where it can be compared, the grammar
and style is uniform in both the Horarium and the Prophecy.
Fourth, Adam is the narrator in both the Horarium and the
Prophecy, and speaks in the first person. Thus, we read at
1:4: "Thus I used to hear, before I sinned, the sound of
their wings in Paradise . . . But after I transgressed against
the law, I did not hear that sound (any longer)," and at 3:1,
"Adam said to his son Seth . . ." Fifth, a common focus on
the first chapters of Genesis constitutes a strong link
between the Horarium and the Prophecy. If one compares the
dramatis personae of Genesis 1 with those of the Horarium, one
finds the following elements common to both: the deep, God's
spirit hovering over the waters, the evening and morning
(night and day), the waters above heaven, the grass of the
earth, the fish, the birds, the beasts, and the creeping
things. In the Horarium, the world is called Creation and God
is called the Creator. Given the strong focus on Creation,
and the abundance of material from Genesis 1 which go to make
up the Horarium, it should not seem odd that it is followed by
a narrative based on Genesis 2-4. In this sense the Prophecy
follows the Horarium quite logically. It is, in fact, the
pattern of several works from the Adam cycle of traditions to
follow the order Creation, Fall and Prophecy in narrating the
career of Adam.[44] While the Horarium and the Prophecy may be
taken ultimately from separate sources, they are compatible
enough to have been drawn together into a single document
because of their common focus in the first chapters of Genesis.

The Hierarchy

Almost every critic who has treated the Testament of
Adam has noted that the Hierarchy is not a part of the original testament. This judgment is supported by the following
facts. The Hierarchy is found in only one late manuscript
of the Syriac Testament of Adam, manuscript C, and is not
found in any of the versions. Also, Adam is not the speaker
in the Hierarchy as he is in the Horarium and Prophecy. The
writer addresses "my beloved" instead of "my son Seth." Moreover, the author refers to several historical events, such as
the defeats of Sennacherib and Antiochus, as past history.
These would be anachronisms in the mouth of Adam. It is also
apparent that the style of the Hierarchy is different from
that of the Horarium and Prophecy in that the latter regularly
use participles without auxiliary verbs or enclitic pronouns,
while the former employs the standard tenses or participles
with auxiliaries or enclitics. Finally, the Hierarchy does
not share the common focus of the Horarium and Prophecy on the
events of Genesis 1-4, and has no connection with the figure
of Adam.

Renan was the first to note the disparate character of
the Hierarchy. He claimed that it was actually an abridgment
of the Celestial Hierarchy of pseudo-Dionysius the Areopagite
and implied that it had been attributed to the Testament of
Adam by scribal error.[45] Although Renan was again followed by
most subsequent critics, he was mistaken on both counts, for
the only similarity between the Hierarchy from the Testament
of Adam and the Celestial Hierarchy of pseudo-Dionysius the
Areopagite is that they both list the traditional nine ranks
of angels and give them the same names.[46] However, the order
in which the ranks are placed is different in the two accounts,
the Hierarchy following the order given in Ephesians 1:21
against the order of pseudo-Dionysius.[47] Further, the function
assigned to each rank is totally different in the two documents, and there are none of the neo-Platonic abstractions in
our document which permeate the account of pseudo-Dionysius.[48]
Much closer parallels to the Hierarchy than that of pseudo-
Dionysius are found in the Book of the Bee by Solomon of Basra,

an account which seems to be dependent upon our document,[49] and in the Cave of Treasures.[50] It appears, therefore, that the Horarium from the Testament of Adam is not merely an abridgment of the Celestial Hierarchy of pseudo-Dionysius the Areopagite.

Beyond this, it should be noted that several passages from the Hierarchy indicate that it was written, or at least redacted, with the Horarium in mind. For example, compare 1:1 with 4:5 in recension 2:

1:1   The first hour of the night is the praise of the waters and of the demons. And in that hour of their praise (they) neither harm nor injure nor destroy anything until dismissed from their praises because a hidden power of the maker of all binds them.

4:5   The fifth order, which is the powers. This is its service: to restrain the demons lest they destroy the creation of God, because of their jealousy toward human beings; because if the accursed nature of demons was allowed to perform the desire of its will, in one hour and a moment they (would) overthrow all creation.

The mention of the hidden power in 1:1 is, like the Hierarchy itself, found only in manuscript C. There can be little doubt that the function of the powers in 4:5 (the Hierarchy) is intended to complement their function in 1:1 (the Horarium), and that the redactor has adapted the reading of the Horarium to accommodate the Hierarchy. Compare also 1:4 and 9 with 4:8,

1:4 The fourth hour: the trishagion of the seraphim.
1:9 The ninth hour: the worship of those angels who (are) standing before the throne of that majesty.

4:8 These other orders, of thrones and seraphim and cherubim, (are) the ones who stand before the majesty of our Lord Jesus the Messiah and serve the throne of his magnificence, glorifying (him) *hourly* with their trishagia.

The functions assigned to the angelic orders in the Hierarchy are intended to complement those found in the Horarium. Undoubtedly, the Hierarchy is an addition to the original Testament of Adam; nevertheless, it is an *intentional* addition edited, at least in part, for the Testament of Adam and has not been attributed to the testament by scribal error.

This leads to the conclusion that, although there are

different levels of redactional activity within the Testament
of Adam, all of the presently extant sections, including the
Hierarchy, were intended by their final redactor to stand as a
unified composition, and that the Testament of Adam should be
considered in each of its three recensions as a single document and not as a mere collection of fragments.

Date

The date of the Testament of Adam has been estimated by
different critics at anywhere between the second and sixth
centuries A.D. While there are exceptions, it may generally
be stated that those scholars who assign a late date to the
Testament of Adam are those who believe it to be dependent
to a greater or lesser extent on the Cave of Treasures,[51]
while most of those who give the testament an early date attribute it to Gnostics.[52] Neither of these views is correct.

Renan and other early critics maintained that there was
only one Gnostic book attributed to Adam in antiquity and
that all known Adamic literature constituted fragments of that
Gnostic work.[53] The term "Testament of Adam" was thencefor-
ward used not merely for our document but for all pseudepigraphical Adamic literature. Using the term in this generic
sense, Renan could maintain that the report by Epiphanius in
the fourth century A.D. of an Apocalypse of Adam in use among
the Gnostics referred to our document even though Epiphanius
never speaks of a "Testament" but always of an "Apocalypse" of
Adam.[54]

Evidently using this same generic definition, R. Duval
reports that much of the "Testament of Adam" is found in the
Cave of Treasures when in fact it is not.[55] Similarly, when
A. Götze discussed the "Testament of Adam" in connection with
the Cave of Treasures and the Conflict of Adam and Eve with
Satan, he did not mean our document, but used the term, as
Renan had, to indicate the Adam tradition generally.[56]

However, when more books from antiquity attributed to
Adam were discovered, it became necessary to abandon Renan's
generic use of the term "Testament of Adam," and most critics
came to reserve the title specifically for our pseudepigraphon.
Nevertheless, in the transition from one definition to the

other many of the judgments of Renan and others about the
"generic" Testament of Adam (Adam literature generally) were
transferred by later scholars to the specific Testament of
Adam. It is not difficult to see how this might happen,
particularly among critics who relied primarily on secondary
sources.

A similar methodological error lies at the base of Hort's
attempt to use the Gelasian Decree to date the Testament of
Adam. The Gelasian Decree does not mention the *testament*, but
rather the *Penitence* of Adam.[57] Hort's dating requires the
equation of non-equivalent terms.

We see then that the criteria which have most commonly
been used in dating the Testament of Adam--its supposed dependence upon the Cave of Treasures or attribution to Gnostics--
involve serious methodological errors. It is necessary to
take a fresh look at the evidence.

The Prophecy

The most helpful piece of objective evidence for dating
the Prophecy is a passage taken from the "Testament of Adam"
found in some Syriac texts of the New Testament apocryphal
work entitled the *Transitus Mariae*, or Assumption of the
Virgin. This document was composed in Greek, perhaps as early
as the late fourth century A.D.,[58] and was soon thereafter
translated into Syriac. The work is mentioned in the Gelasian
Decree, which E. von Dobschütz dates in the early sixth century A.D.[59]

A Syriac palimpsest published by A. Smith Lewis has as
the under writing a copy of the *Transitus Mariae* in Syriac
which dates from the late fifth century and contains the
following:

> Our father Adam when dying commanded his son Seth,
> and said to him, "My son Seth, lo, offerings are
> laid up by me in the cave of treasures; gold, and
> myrrh, and frankincense; because God is about to come
> into the world, and to be seized by wicked men, and to
> die, and make by His death a resurrection for all
> nations; and on the third day He will rise, and will
> take the body of Adam with Him to heaven, and will
> make it sit on the right hand. And lo! the Magi are
> coming from Persia, and will go to Bethlehem of Judah
> and worship the Messiah, who is born there of the
> holy Virgin. And so it was. And the Magi came and

brought the offerings, and they brought the testament
of Adam with them. And from the testament of Adam
all mankind have learned to make testaments; and from
the Messiah, who was born of Mary, all mankind who
were in darkness, have been enlightened. And thus
from Adam to Seth writing was used; and from Seth
letters were written, to the fathers gave [them]
the sons; and the sons gave [them] to the sons' sons;
and they said that 'The Messiah shall come and shall
be born of Mary the Virgin in Bethlehem.'"[60]

Two manuscripts of the same work edited by W. Wright,
British Museum Additional manuscripts 14,484 and 14,732, contain essentially the same passage, and are dated to the sixth
century.[61] It would have required some time for the Prophecy
to have circulated sufficiently in Syriac to be used as a
source by the *Transitus Mariae* in the fifth century. This
suggests a *terminus ad quem* not later than the end of the
fourth century for the composition of the Prophecy.[62] Since
the Prophecy is clearly Christian in its present form and is
dependent upon traditions found in the New Testament, such as
the birth of Jesus at Bethlehem and the visit of the Magi, the
terminus a quo probably should not be placed before the early
decades of the second century.

Between these two limits, the Prophecy section of the
Testament of Adam can be placed more exactly by analyzing the
importance of a parallel passage in the Apocalypse of Elijah.
The passage from the Testament of Adam which describes the
activities of the coming Messiah at 3:1 is also found in the
Apocalypse of Elijah at 33:1-8. However, in the Apocalypse of
Elijah it has been adapted as a description of the deceiving
wonders which the Antichrist will perform. The passage from
the Testament of Adam reads:

> . . . walking on the waves of the sea as upon boards
> of wood, rebuking the winds and (they are) silenced,
> beckoning to the waves and (they are) still; also
> opening (the eyes of) the blind and cleansing the
> lepers, and causing the deaf to hear. And the mute
> speak. And (he is) casting out evil spirits, and
> driving out demons, and restoring the dead to life,
> and raising the buried from the midst of their
> graves.[63]

The passage from the Apocalypse reads:

> He will walk upon the sea and the rivers as upon dry
> land. He will cause the lame to walk. He will cause

the deaf to hear. He will cause the dumb to speak.
He will cause the blind to see. The lepers he will
cleanse. The ill he will heal. The demons he will
cast out. He will multiply his signs and his wonders
in the presence of everyone. He will do the works
which the Christ did, except for raising the dead
alone.[64]

It will be noted that the Apocalypse of Elijah denies to the
Antichrist the power to raise the dead which is attributed to
the Messiah in the passage from the Testament of Adam. This
specific exception may indicate that the Apocalypse of Elijah
is adapting a traditional list of messianic signs and wonders
to fit its description of the Antichrist. It is more likely
that a messianic list would be adapted to fit the Antichrist
than that the characteristics of the Antichrist would be
applied to the Messiah; hence, it appears that the Prophecy
from the Testament of Adam preserves this passage in a more
original form than does the Apocalypse of Elijah. Although
it is impossible to tell whether the Apocalypse of Elijah is
directly dependent upon the Testament of Adam, or whether both
documents take the passage from a common source, it is significant that the form of the passage in the Testament of Adam
is the more original because the Apocalypse of Elijah is usually dated in the third century A.D.

Since the "Testament of Adam" is cited in a fifth century
manuscript of the Syriac *Transitus Mariae*, and since one of
its most Christian, and therefore latest, passages is either
the source of, or at least prior in form to the third century
Apocalypse of Elijah, it is not unreasonable to tentatively
date the Syriac Testament of Adam to the third century A.D.
This estimate roughly splits the difference between the two
limits on the one hand, and yet recognizes the evidence
afforded by the Apocalypse of Elijah on the other.[65]

The Horarium

As we shall see below,[66] the Horarium was originally a
Jewish document which has been adapted by the Christian redactor of the Testament of Adam to introduce the Prophecy of Adam
to Seth. It seems likely, therefore, that in this case, as in
the Pseudepigrapha generally, the Jewish stratum is earlier
than its Christian accretions. If we assume that the redactor

who was responsible for the Christian elements of the Prophecy
was also responsible for combining the Prophecy with the
Horarium, as seems likely, then the "Testament of Adam" refer-
red to in the *Transitus Mariae* must already have included the
Horarium and the Horarium cannot be dated any later than the
Prophecy, though it may be dated earlier.

If, on the other hand, the Horarium and Prophecy circulated independently, there is no evidence to indicate when
they might have been joined together other than the manuscripts themselves, which date from the ninth century. But
since it is generally the case that when Jewish and Christian
elements are found together, the Jewish elements are earlier
than the Christian, we find it probable that the Horarium,
like the Prophecy, should be dated no later than the fifth
century, and in all probability no later than the third
century, although it may be earlier.

A significant argument for a relatively early date for
the Horarium was first proposed by M. R. James. James maintained that the *Inquisitio Abrae* mentioned by Nicetas of
Remesiana ought to be read *Dispositio Adae*, and that it was
in fact a Latin version of the Testament of Adam.[67] James
thought this proposal would necessitate at least a fourth
century date for the Latin testament since Nicetas died about
A.D. 414.[68] If James is right, his hypothesis would necessitate a still earlier date for the Syriac text, perhaps as
early as the late third or early fourth century. However,
James' hypothesis cannot be proved, and although the existence
of a Latin Testament of Adam is a distinct possibility, it is
only a possiblity and cannot be used in dating the Horarium.
The contention of F. Nau that the Horarium was composed in the
first century A.D. is dependent upon his assertion, now discredited,[69] that it was written by Apollonius of Tyana, and
has no concrete evidence to commend it.

The Hierarchy

It is presently impossible to date the Hierarchy except
within very broad limits. It is found in an early eighteenth
century manuscript of the Tesatment of Adam (manuscript C).
Solomon of Basra used a form of the Hierarchy which appears to
be less Jewish than that from the Testament of Adam in his

thirteenth century Book of the Bee.[70] The Hierarchy has a
great deal in common with the angelology of pseudo-Dionysius
the Areopagite, with that of the Cave of Treasures, which may
date to as early as the second century, and with those found
in the New Testament and in the Pseudepigrapha.[71] It may
represent an original Jewish angelology from the late intertestamental period which has survived because of its slight
Christian interpolations; but this is suggested only as a
possibility. In the absence of further evidence, the date of
the Hierarchy, even in general terms, remains uncertain.

Conclusion

By way of summary, let us now draw together some of the
conclusions relative to the date of the testament which have
been discussed above and in previous chapters.[72] The Prophecy
from the Testament of Adam probably dates from the third
century A.D. This tentative date is suggested by its dependence upon Christian traditions found in the New Testament,
by its being used as a source for the Syriac *Transitus Mariae*,
and by its affinities with the third century Apocalypse of
Elijah. It is likely that the Christian redactor of the
Prophecy also combined the Prophecy with the Horarium, which
should probably also be dated no later than the third century
A.D. The Hierarchy cannot presently be dated to a specific
period, though we must be open to the possibility that the
traditions found there may date from a very early period,
perhaps even from intertestamental times.

The Arabic version of the testament is dependent upon the
Syriac and was probably composed no earlier than the eighth
century A.D.[73] The Ethiopic version is dependent upon and
later than the Arabic. The Greek version is also dependent
upon the Syriac and cannot be dated earlier than the tenth
century A.D.[74]

The Provenience of the Testament of Adam

The final task of the present study is to define the
character of the Testament of Adam; that is, to determine the
religious environment which produced the final document and
each of its component parts. Some of this task has already
been accomplished above in relation to other critical issues;

these conclusions will be repeated here and combined with
additional observations. No less than four different religious environments have been suggested as the native theological
soil out of which the Tesatment of Adam grew. These are
Greek and Roman paganism, Gnosticism, Christianity, and
Judaism. We will examine the case for each of these in turn.

Greek and Roman Paganism

The possibility that the Testament of Adam was the work
of a pagan author was suggested by F. Nau in 1907.[75] Nau
contended that the Greek version of the testament, which consists solely of the Horarium, is the original and that it was
composed in the first century by the famous magician and
philosopher Apollonius of Tyana. His argument rests basically
on two main points: one, that the larger work that contains
the Greek Horarium, the *Apotelesmata*, is attributed in three
of the six manuscripts to Apollonius; and two, that the
Apotelesmata is just the kind of magical treatise that one
would expect Apollonius to have written judging from the
extant traditional information about him. Nau explained the
biblical elements found in the Horarium as later Christian
interpolations, and insisted that the Prophecy from the
Testament of Adam was a much later addition to the Horarium
taken from the Cave of Treasures.

Nau's theory found few supporters, even in his own day.
Among several overwhelming objections to his thesis are the
following. First, the Greek version is not earlier than the
tenth century. Second, given the late date of the Greek, it
is more likely that the magical nature of the text influenced
its attribution to Apollonius than that Apollonius actually
wrote it. Third, the Greek is dependent upon the Syriac.
Finally, the biblical elements in the Greek version are too
pervasive to be explained away as a Christian varnish. Indeed,
they are so woven into the fabric of the document that it is
inconceivable that it was composed by a pagan.[76]

Gnosticism

From its first critical appraisal in 1853 until the
present, there have been those scholars who attributed authorship of the Testament of Adam to the Gnostics, or at least to

Gnostic influence. This idea is, next to the belief that the
testament is dependent upon the Cave of Treasures, perhaps the
most widespread critical misconception about the document.[77]

   This mistaken assessment can largely be traced to the
methodological error of early critics like Renan and Hort who
equated the Testament of Adam with the Apocalypse of Adam
attributed by Epiphanius to the Gnostics. The term Gnosticism
had a broader extension as used by Renan than it does when
used by modern critics. As used by Renan, "Gnosticism" was a
blanket term for almost any strange or unusual (from Renan's
perspective) form of Christianity and, indeed, was almost a
synonym for "heterodoxy." However, since the time of W. Bauer,
and particularly since the discovery of the Nag Hammadi
Codices, it has been necessary to show greater caution in the
use of the terms "orthodoxy," "heresy," and "Gnosticism."[78]
It is no longer permissible as it was in Renan's day to use
"Gnosticism" as an open category into which one may pour all
the remains of little-known or little-understood varieties of
Christianity.

   This is not to imply that there is today a universally
accepted definition for the term "gnosticism." However, there
has been a tremendous narrowing of the general limits to which
the term can be stretched;[79] and even if one adopts a comparatively broad definition of the term, in terms of modern critical views, it is clear that the Testament of Adam cannot be
called a product of gnosticism.

   In fact, one might say with J. B. Frey that the Testament
of Adam is even "anti-Gnostic."[80] There are several compel-
ling reasons why the Testament of Adam cannot be considered
a Gnostic document. First, there is no evidence to connect
the Testament of Adam with the Gnostic systems of the second
century other than the ill-advised equation of the Testament
and Apocalypse of Adam. Second, the fall of man in the Testament of Adam is completely intra-mundane; there is no devolu-
tion from a higher realm; Adam is made entirely from the dust
of the earth as in Genesis 1, and there is no divine spark
captured within him. Adam's divinity is a prospect entirely
for the future. Third, the promised salvation is to be
accomplished solely through the person of Jesus the Messiah,

who is not portrayed as a descending Revealer-Redeemer.   There
is no mention of salvation by gnosis.   Fourth, there is neither an anticosmic nor a metaphysical dualism.   The Horarium
emphasizes the unity of all creation, angels and devils alike,
in rendering praises to God.   The whole focus of the document
is the proper glorification of the Creator by a worshipful
creation.   Fifth, there is nothing secret about the information which Adam passes on to Seth, nor is the revelation
couched in the vocabulary typical of second century Gnostic
systems.[81]   The concept of revelation in the Testament of Adam
is entirely "biblical."   Finally, the Testament of Adam manifests a deep respect for the Old Testament and for Jewish
traditions generally.   It is by no means anti-Jewish.

The Testament of Adam is not a Gnostic document.   The
mistaken view to the contrary is attributable to three factors:
an outmoded definition of Gnosticism; the incorrect assumption
that all Adam compositions are parts of a single book; and
the repetition in recent secondary literature of opinions that
are frequently over one hundred years old.

Christianity and Judaism

The Horarium

There can be no doubt that the Testament of Adam in its
present form is a Christian document.   The references to the
figure of Christ are obvious and explicit.   These passages are
found at 1:1 (recension 2 only), 3:1, 3:3b, 3:4, 3:7b (not
found in recension 2), 3:8 (recension 3 only), 4:1 and 4:8
(both in recension 2 only).   A mere listing of these occurrences discloses an interesting clustering: with the exception
of the scribal gloss in 1:1 of recension 2, there are no indis-
putably Christian elements in the Horarium.   All of the
Christian passages occur in the Prophecy of Adam to Seth or in
the Hierarchy.   This striking disparity between the Horarium
and the Prophecy may indicate that the Horarium represents a
Jewish source out of which the final document was constructed.
In addition to the lack of Christian elements in the Horarium,
this hypothesis is supported by the following considerations.
First, the Horarium, unlike the Prophecy, shares at least two
characteristics with Jewish Wisdom literature.   Perhaps the

most pronounced of these is an interest in the order of creation.
As M. Hengel states:

> An important preparation for the encounter of Jewish
> wisdom teaching with Greek thought was that it had
> become more and more bound up with the doctrine of
> creation. . . . This connection of wisdom with the
> doctrine of creation had a twofold consequence. On
> the one hand it led to an encyclopaedic treatment of
> all the phenomena in the world created by God. Here
> the ordering of creation and the functioning of its
> offshoots were not, of course, understood as an
> immanent 'natural' process--this conception was alien
> to early Jewish wisdom--but as a divine miracle.[82]

Hengel's description of this particular focus of Jewish wisdom
literature as it began its encounter with Greek thought
closely approximates the spirit behind the composition of the
Horarium. Moreover, G. von Rad, in discussing the concept of
time in Wisdom literature might just as well be describing the
intellectual orientation which produced the Horarium. He
writes:

> The tree yields its fruit "in its time" (Ps. I.3),
> and God gives his creatures food "in due time" (Ps.
> CIV.27); that is to say, every event had its defi-
> nite place in the time-order; the event is incon-
> ceivable without its time, and *vice versa*.[83]

In the Horarium, the preoccupation with creation and the belief
in the "divine determination of times" are brought together in
a unique synthesis.

Second, although the Prophecy and Horarium share a focus
in the first chapters of Genesis, they are otherwise almost
totally unrelated. Events from the lives of the Patriarchs
are ignored in the Horarium. Also, when the Horarium is represented as being spoken by Adam several anachronisms appear,
particularly concerning the activities of the priests in
anointing the sick and offering incense.

Third, in contrast to the Prophecy, the scriptural affinities of the Horarium lie solidly and exclusively with the
Old Testament. The following allusions and parallels should
be noted: 1:3 (Ps 148:7-8), 1:4 (Isa 6:1-6 and Ezek 3:13),
1:5 (Gen 1:7-8, Ps 148:4 and Ezek 1:24), 1:12 (Ps 104:4),
2:1-2 (Ps 148:1-2), 2:10 (Gen 1:2). Certainly the activity
depicted in the Horarium, the worship of the Creator by his
creation, is in keeping with the injunction of Psalm 145:21;

"Yahweh's praise be ever in my mouth, and let every creature bless his holy name forever and ever." Psalm 150:6 enjoins: "Let everything that breathes praise Yahweh!" Further, the parallels between the opening verses of the Horarium (recension 1) and Psalm 148:1-8 are close enough to suggest literary dependence:

> Praise the Lord! Praise the Lord from the heavens, praise him in the heights! Praise him, all his angels, praise him, all his host! Praise him, sun and moon, praise him, all you shining stars! Praise him you highest heavens, and you waters above the heavens! Let them praise the name of the Lord! For he commanded and they were created. And he established them for ever and ever; he fixed their bounds which cannot be passed. Praise the Lord from the earth, you sea monsters and all deeps, fire and hail . . . (Ps 148:1-8a)

Finally, the whole idea of the Creator being praised hourly by his creation is thoroughly Jewish. No less an authority than L. Ginzberg has written:

> The conception that the animals and all created things chant praise to God is genuinely Jewish, and is not only poetically expressed in the Bible (Ps. 65.14, etc.), but occurs quite frequently in talmudic and midrashic literature, where the "singing" and praise of the animals and trees are spoken of; comp. Rosh ha-Shanah 8a; Hullin 54b; 'Abodah Zarah 24b; BR 13.2; Tehillim 104, 442-443 . . . and 148, 538.[84]

We conclude, therefore, that the Horarium was probably an independent Jewish composition which was used by the Christian redactor of the Testament of Adam as a preface for the Prophecy because of its common focus with it on the first chapters of Genesis.

The Prophecy

The Prophecy contains several bits of tradition that are of Jewish origin, though not found in the Old Testament, and whose presence in the Christian Testament of Adam cannot therefore be explained by the common scriptural heritage of Judaism and Christianity. The traditions about Adam's prediction of the Flood (3:5),[85] the death and burial of Adam (3:6),[86] the sister of Cain and Abel (3:5),[87] the fig as the forbidden fruit (3:4a, rec. 2),[88] and the city of Enoch (3:6),[89] are all thoroughly Jewish in origin. Therefore the Prophecy must

either be a Christian work shaped out of earlier Jewish tradi-
tions, or an originally Jewish document with several long
Christian interpolations. If we eliminate the obvious scribal
gloss in 1:1 of recension 2 and the three occurrences of "our
Lord Jesus the Messiah" or "our Lord" found in the added
Hierarchy (also from rec. 2), we see that there are only four
such possible interpolations in the entire Testament of Adam.[90]
This observation further suggests the possibility that the
Prophecy may be a heavily redacted Jewish composition rather
than a Christian work which incorporates Jewish ideas.

The Hierarchy

The Hierarchy from the Testament of Adam is the most
neglected section of a neglected document. Since it was not a
part of the original testament and since it is found in only
one eighteenth century manuscript, it has been deemed a very
late Christian composition. It has also been attributed,
incorrectly, to pseudo-Dionysius the Areopagite. The fact
that it has much more in common with the angelologies of the
New Testament and of the Books of Enoch[91] than with pseudo-
Dionysius, a fact which may indicate a date before the fifth
century A.D.,[92] has been repeatedly overlooked. More important, however, is the fact that the only necessarily Christian
element of the entire Hierarchy are the titles "our Lord Jesus
the Messiah" or just "our Lord" found in 4:1 and 4:8. The
temptation to emend these to read simply "the Lord" is very
inviting, for by doing so we would be left with an angelology
very similar to others from intertestamental times, and one
which has no identifiable Christian characteristics.

An example of Jewish material which has received just
this type of minimal Christian interpolation is found in the
Sixteen Synagogal Hymns from the Apostolic Constitutions. In
these hymns, Jewish liturgical material has been adapted for
Christian audiences.[93] In the first hymn, for example, the
line "We give thanks to you, O God and Father," has received
an appositional interpolation to read "We give thanks to you,
O God and Father *of Jesus our Savior*."[94] The sixth hymn
closes with a similarly interpolated passage:

> And now, therefore, receive the prayers of your
> people,
> Offered up with full knowledge to you *through Christ,
> in the Spirit*.[95]

As in the Hierarchy from the Testament of Adam, the only
Christian elements involve the appositional interpolation of
divine names and titles.

We therefore suggest, rather cautiously, that the Hierarchy may represent an originally Jewish angelology which has
been adapted for a Christian audience by the substitution of
"our Lord" for "the Lord" followed by the appositional interpolation "Jesus the Messiah." This work was then appended to
one recension of the Testament of Adam. This same angelology
was further christianized by Solomon of Basra in the thirteenth century by the removal of its Old Testament and Jewish
apocryphal references.[96]

Conclusion

The Testament of Adam is in its present form the work of
a Christian redactor who used earlier Jewish sources to piece
together the present work. The Horarium is entirely Jewish
and has very strong affinities with Genesis 1 and Psalm 148.
It was apparently joined to the Prophecy because its focus
on the themes of creation and praise of the Creator was deemed
compatible with the figure of Adam. The Prophecy is either a
Christian composition whose author relied heavily on Jewish
traditions, or more likely an originally Jewish composition
which has been substantially redacted by Christians. The
Hierarchy, which was not a part of the original testament, may
be a traditional Jewish angelology purposely added to the testament because it complemented the angelology implied in the
Horarium.

CONCLUSION

Respectus

This study of the Testament of Adam has reached several conclusions concerning both the testament itself and the discussions of earlier critics. The nine major conclusions have been assembled for convenience and are listed below in the order in which they appear in the body of the text:

1. The Testament of Adam is one of several independent compositions from antiquity attributed to the figure of Adam.

2. This Adam-cycle of literature should be treated as a collection of separate but related compositions, and not as diverse fragments of a single work.

3. Because of the erroneous conclusions of early critics about the Testament of Adam, the document has been unreasonably neglected; only one major treatment of it has appeared in the last fifty years.

4. This same half century has witnessed a considerable change in the critical perspective of scholars relative to Judaism, Christianity, and Gnosticism.

5. This change in critical perspective calls for a re-evaluation of the Pseudepigrapha in general, including the Testament of Adam.

6. The original language of the Testament of Adam is Syriac.

7. The extant Testament of Adam was intended by the final redactor of each recension to form a literary unity.

8. The Prophecy should probably be dated in the third century; the Horarium is at least that early, and perhaps earlier; the Hierarchy, though certainly composed before the thirteenth century and perhaps before the fifth, cannot be dated more precisely than this with any degree of certainty.

9. The Horarium appears to be an originally Jewish
    composition; the Prophecy is either a Christian
    composition or a Jewish work heavily interpolated;
    the Hierarchy may be a Jewish work with slight
    Christian interpolation.

Prospectus

Perhaps the most intriguing question left unexamined
revolves around the figure of Seth and his role in the testament. It has become increasingly apparent that Seth enjoyed
a more signficant role in Jewish and Christian thought than
previously supposed. The role of Seth in the Testament of
Adam may provide an insight into his broader importance in
Jewish, Christian and Gnostic circles, and help establish his
importance in a non-Gnostic Sethian tradition. Moreover, our
understanding of how Adam himself was perceived in the first
centuries of this era may be significantly enhanced by an
examination of the testament along lines similar to those
recently pursued by R. Scroggs. This in turn may shed light
on our understanding of the figure of Adam in the New Testament.

We have not attempted to discuss the theology of the
Testament of Adam. It is hoped that a future examination in
this area will provide supporting evidence for the date of
the testament, particularly in connection with the theme of
Adam's deification.

Finally, it is hoped that the Arabic, Ethiopic, Karshuni,
Old Georgian and Armenian versions of the Testament of Adam
will be subjected to a similar re-evaluation, and that the
judgments of A Götze, Z. Avalachvili, S. Grebaut and others
may be re-evaluated.

NOTE TO INTRODUCTION

1. See R. Murray, *Symbols of Church and Kingdom* (Cambridge: Cambridge University Press, 1975). As judged by the early critics, the Testament of Adam would lay outside the scope of Murray's work.

NOTES TO CHAPTER I

1. Cf. M. Eliade, *The Myth of the Eternal Return or Cosmos and History*, trans. W. R. Trask (Princeton: Princeton University Press, 1974), p. 4.

2. 1Tim 2:11-15.

3. Matt 19:8.

4. G. H. Box, "4 Ezra," *APOT*, vol. 2, p. 591.

5. R. H. Charles, "2 Baruch," *APOT*, vol. 2, pp. 511-12.

6. G. H. Box, *APOT*, vol. 2, p. 553f.

7. J. B. Frey, "Adam (Livres apocryphes sous son nom)," *Dictionnaire de la Bible, Supplément* (Paris: Letouzey et Ané, 1928), vol. 1, col. 101.

8. See below pp. 17-18.

9. A. Roberts and J. Donaldson, eds., *The Ante-Nicene Fathers* (Grand Rapids, Mich.: Wm. B. Eerdmans Publishing Co., 1975), vol. 7, p. 457.

10. L. Zunz, *Göttesdienstliche Vorträge der Jüden* (Berlin: A. Asher, 1832), pp. 128-29.

11. A. Cohen, *The Babylonian Talmud: Abodah Zarah* (London: Soncino, 1935), pp. 19-20.

12. H. Freedman, *Midrash Rabbah: Genesis* (London: Soncino, 1939), p. 200. See also the very similar allusions at Gen. R. 24:3 and 24:4.

13. S. M. Lehrman, *Midrash Rabbah: Exodus* (London: Soncino, 1939), p. 461.

14. H. Freedman, *The Babylonian Talmud: Baba Mezia* (London: Soncino, 1935), pp. 492-93.

15. L. Ginzberg, "Adam, Book of," *The Jewish Encyclopedia* (New York: Funk and Wagnalls Co., 1901), vol. 1, p. 179.

16. Ibid., p. 180.

17. J. P. Migne, *PG* 89:35-1288. The list of "Sixty Books" is dated at about the beginning of the eighth century.

18. M. E. Stone, "Armenian Canon Lists III--the Lists of Mechitar of Ayrivank (c. 1285 C.E.)," *HTR* 69 (1976) 289-300. For treatment of the ancient references to the books of Adam generally, see M. R. James, *The Lost Apocrypha of the Old Testament* (New York: Macmillan, 1920), pp. xi-xiv, 1-4; and A. M. Denis, *Introduction aux Pseudepigraphes Grecs d'Ancien Testament* (SVTP 1; Leiden: E.J. Brill, 1970), pp. xi, 3-14.

19. H. S. Josepheanz, *The Uncanonical Books of the Old Testament* [Armenian] (Venice: Library of St. Lazarus, 1896), trans. J. Issaverdens, *The Uncanonical Writings of the Old Testament* (Venice: Armenian Monastery of St. Lazarus, 1901).

20. Issaverdens, *The Uncanonical Writings*, p. 11.

21. See below pp. 148-49, 155.

22. Migne, *PG* 89:967.

23. Frey, *Dictionnaire de la Bible, Supplément*, vol. 1, col. 123.

24. Epiphanius, *Panarion,* 26.3; see K. Holl, ed., *Epiphanius: Ancoratus und Panarion* (Leipzig: J.C. Hinrichs, 1915).

25. A. Böhlig and P. Labib, *Koptisch-gnostiche Apokalypsen aus Codex V von Nag Hammadi im Koptischen Museum zu Alt-Kairo* (Halle: Martin-Luther-Universität, 1963).

26. E.g. the story of the twin pillars of Seth, *Ant.* 1.2.3.

27. See G. W. MacRae and D. M. Parrott, "The Apocalypse of Adam (V, 5)," in *The Nag Hammadi Library*, ed. J. M. Robinson (San Francisco: Harper & Row, Publishers, 1977), pp. 256-64.

28. K. Lake, *The Apostolic Fathers* (LCL; New York: G.P. Putnam's Sons, 1930), vol. 1, p. 345.

29. Irenaeus, *Against Heresies*, 4.17.2 (*ANF*, vol. 1, p. 483); Clement of Alexandria, *The Instructor*, 31.12 and *Miscellanies*, 2.18 (*ANF*, vol. 2, pp. 293, 365).

30. Denis, *Introduction*, p. 11, identifies this manuscript as "ms. Conspl. Panag. Taphous 54 (aujourd'hui au Métoque de Jérusalem), *anno* 1056."

31. James, *Lost Apocrypha*, p. 1.

32. E. von Dobschütz, "Das Decretum Gelasianum," *Texte und Untersuchungen* 38 (1912) 338-48.

33. Ibid., p. 12.

34. J. A. Hort, "Adam, Books of," *Dictionary of Christian Biography*, W. Smith and H. Wace, eds. (London: John Murray, 1977), vol. 1, pp. 37-8. Also, see a Latin version of the text in Migne, *PG* 19:686.

35. Hort, *Dictionary of Christian Biography*, vol. 1, pp. 38-9, and R. H. Charles, "The Book of Jubilees," *APOT*, vol. 2, p. 2.

36. Frey, *Dictionnaire de la Bible, Supplément*, vol. 1, cols. 133-34; and E. Schürer, *A History of the Jewish People in the Time of Jesus Christ*, trans. S. Taylor and P. Christie (Edinburgh: T.&T. Clark, 1924), div. 2, vol. 3, p. 140.

37. George Syncellus, *Chronographia* 1.7-9; see G. Dindorf, *George Syncellus et Nicephorus Cp.*, vol. 1, p. 7, in *Corpus Scriptorum Historiae Byzantinae* (Bonn: Weber, 1829).

38. W. Meyer, "Vita Adae et Evae," *Abhandlungen der bayerischen Akademie der Wissenschaften*, philos.-philol. Klasse, 14.3 (Munich, 1878), pp. 185-250.

39. C. Tischendorf, *Apocalypses Apocryphae* (Leipzig, 1866; reprint ed., George Olms Hildesheim, 1966), pp. x-xii, 1-23.

40. C. Bezold, *Die Schatzhöhle* (Leipzig: J.C. Hinrichs, 1183/8).

41. E. A. W. Budge, *The Book of the Cave of Treasures* (London: Religious Tract Society, 1927).

42. See M. D. Gibson, *Apocrypha Arabica* (Studia Sinaitica 8; London, 1901), pp. 1-58.

43. Cf. A. Götze, "Die Schatzhöhle, Überlieferungen und Quellen," *Sitzungsberichte der Heidelberger Akademie der Wissenschaften*, philos.-hist. Klasse, 1922, pp. 90-1. See also Budge, *The Cave of Treasures*, pp. 21-2.

44. A. Dillmann, *Das christliche Adambuch des Orients* (Göttingen: Dieterich, 1853).

45. S. C. Malan, *The Book of Adam and Eve* (London: Williams and Norgate, 1882).

46. See M. Stone, "The Death of Adam--An Armenian Adam Book," *HTR* 55 (1966) 283-91.

47. See I. Bekker, *George Cedrenus*, vol. 1, pp. 17-8, in *Corpus Scriptorum Historiae Byzantinae* (Bonn: Weber,

1828); see also Migne, *PG* 121:41. Another Byzantine chronicler, George Syncellus, had alluded to this work, but did not cite it, 200 years earlier. See Dindorf, *George Syncellus*, vol. 1, p. 18.

48. A. Smith Lewis, *Apocrypha Syriaca* (Studia Sinaitica 11; London: C.J. Clay & Sons, 1902), p. 41.

49. See below pp. 128-29.

50. See below pp. 52-59, 110-27.

51. M. R. James, "Notes on Apocrypha," *JTS* 7 (1906) 562-63.

52. Ibid., p. 563.

53. Frey, *Dictionnaire de la Bible, Supplément*, vol. 1, col. 123, and E. Schürer, *Geschichte des judischen Volkes im Zeitalter Jesu Christi* (Leipzig, 1901/9), vol. 3, p. 337.

54. A. E. Burn, *Niceta of Remesiana, His Life and Works* (Cambridge: Cambridge University Press, 1905), pp. lxxxvii-lxxxix, 70-1.

55. *Bullettino di archeologia cristiana*, 1877, pl. 5. Note also H. Leclercq's misrendering of the caption in *Dictionnaire d'archeologie chrétienne et de liturgie* (Paris: Letouzey et Ané, 1924), vol. 1, col. 515.

56. Cited by T. I. Schmidt in *Bull. Instit. Archeol. russe a Constple* 8 (1893) 266, n. 4.

57. Denis, *Introduction*, pp. 9-10; see also John Chrysostum in *PG* 56:527.

58. Tabari, *Annals*, I, 76, 7ff; and 79, 14ff.

59. Translated into Latin from the Arabic by H. Dalmata in T. Bibliander, *Alcoran* (Zurich, 1563), pp. 201-12. See also the note of R. Strothmann concerning this tradition in relation to the Syriac Cave of Treasures in his review of Götze's "Die Schatzhohle" in *Der Islam* 13 (1923) 304-07.

60. Migne, *PG* 122:846 n. 70 and 853 n. 91.

61. E.g. E. Renan, "Fragments du livre Gnostique intitulé Apocalypse d'Adam, ou Pénitence d'Adam ou Testament d'Adam," *JA* 5.2 (1853) 427-71, especially pp. 428-29.

62. M. R. James, *Apocrypha Anecdota II*, ed. J. A. Robinson (Texts and Studies 5, Cambridge: Cambridge University Press, 1897), p. lxxxiii.

63. M. R. James, "Apocrypha," in *Encyclopedia Biblica* (New York: Macmillan, 1899), vol. 1, col. 253. See also the similar equation of L. S. A. Wells, "The Books of Adam and Eve," in *APOT*, vol. 2, p. 125, in which the Testament, Apocalypse and Penitence are all compressed into a single Gnostic document.

64. CG V, 5. See MacRae and Parrot, "The Apocalypse of Adam (V, 5)," p. 256.

65. Denis, *Introduction*, pp. 3-14.

66. See below pp. 146-48.

67. M. Kmosko, "Testamentum Adae," *PS*, vol. 2, pp. 1309-60.

68. Except in Old Georgian. See M. D. Gibson, *Apocrypha Arabica*, E. Bratke, "Handschriftliche Überlieferung und Bruchstücke der arabische-aethiopischen Petrusapokalypse," *ZWT* 1 (1893) 454-93; and Z. Avalachvili, "Notice sur une Version Géorgienne de la Caverne des Trésors," *ROC* 26 (1928) 381-405.

69. W. Wright, *A Short History of Syriac Literature* (London, 1894; reprint ed., Amsterdam: Philo Press, 1966), p. 25, n. 2, and A. Götze, "Die Nachwirkung der Schatzhöhle," *ZSVG* 2 (1924) 92.

70. Vatican Syriac MS 164, and British Museum Add. MS 25,815.

71. A. Götze, "Die Schatzhöhle," p. 23.

72. Götze, *ZSVG* 2 (1924) 92.

NOTES TO CHAPTER II

1. J. S. Assemani, *Bibliotheca Orientalis* (Rome, 1725), vol. 3, pt. 1, p. 282.

2. Renan, *JA* 5.2 (1853) 427-71

3. Renan did not hear of Dillmann's work on the Combat of Adam and Eve with Satan until after his own article was completed; cf. Renan, *JA* 5.2 (1853) 427-71, and Dillmann, *Das christliche Adambuch des Orients*.

4. Renan, *JA* 5.2 (1853) 431.

5. Cf. G. J. Reinink, "Das Problem des Ursprungs des Testamentes Adams," *OCA* 197 (1972) 397. See below pp. for text.

6. Reinink, *OCA* 197 (1972) 397.

7. See Frey's argument on this point, *Dictionnaire de la Bible, Supplément*, vol. 1, cols. 122-23.

8. Renan, *JA* 5.2 (1853) 435.

9. Ibid., pp. 435-36, although several of these elements are not as pronounced as Renan maintained. For a further discussion see below, pp. 154-56. See also Frey, *Dictionnaire de la Bible, Supplément*, vol. 1, col. 122.

10. Among those scholars who have suggested a Gnostic origin for the Testament of Adam are Renan, Bezold, Wells, Götze, Leclercq and Cardona. Much of this thinking has been influenced by E. Preuschen's theory of Gnostic origins for the Armenian Adam books; see *Die apokryphen gnostischen Adamschriften* (Giessen: Ricker, 1900), pp. 60-90.

11. Hort, *Dictionary of Christian Biography*, vol. 1, pp. 34-9.

12. Ibid., p. 37.

13. Ibid., p. 38.

14. Ibid.

15. Renan, *JA* 5.2 (1853) 430, attributed the Testament of Adam to "fractions les moins épurées du christianisme oriental."

16. Hort, *Dictionary of Christian Biography*, vol. 1, p. 38.

17. M. R. James, *The Testament of Abraham* (Texts and Studies

2.2; Cambridge: University Press, 1892), p. 121. This
obscure reference is cited incorrectly in James' better
known article *A Fragment of the Apocalypse of Adam in
Greek* (Texts and Studies 2.3; 1892), p. 138, n. 1, as
occurring in Texts and Studies 2.2, 127.

18. James, *A Fragment of the Apocalypse of Adam*, p. 145.

19. James, *JTS* 7 (1906) 562-63.

20. James, *Lost Apocrypha*, p. 41.

21. Ibid., p. 3.

22. Ibid., p. 4.

23. C. Bezold, "Das arabisch-äthiopische Testamentum Adami,"
     *Orientalische Studien Theodor Nöldeke zum Siebzigsten
     Geburtstag* (Giessen: Topelmann, 1906), vol. 2, pp. 893-
     912.

24. Budge, *The Cave of Treasures*, pp. 242ff. The Syriac
     text of the Testament of Adam has never before been
     translated into English.

25. Bezold mentions that a colleague had referred him to the
     article in Texts and Studies 2.2, but he repeatedly
     attributes the article to W. E. Barnes.

26. Bezold, *Orientalische Studien*, pp. 895, 909-11.

27. M. Kmosko, "Testamentum Adae," *PS*, vol. 2, pp. 1309-60.

28. Renan did, of course, use four Arabic MSS in support of
     the two Syriac MSS.

29. It should be noted that when Kmosko wrote, terms like
     "orthodoxy" and "superstition" were in common use to
     describe early Christianity. Today, thanks particularly
     to the efforts of W. Bauer, it is recognized that use of
     such terms represents prejudicial and uncritical assump-
     tions. See W. Bauer, *Orthodoxy and Heresy in Earliest
     Christianity* (Philadelphia: Fortress, 1971).

30. F. Nau, "Apotelesmata Apollonii Tyanensis," *PS*, vol. 2,
     pp. 1363-85.

31. See Frey, *Dictionnaire de la Bible, Supplément*, vol. 1,
     cols. 118-19, 121-22; James, *Lost Apocrypha*, pp. 2-3; and
     below pp. 137-39, 154.

32. Götze, "Die Schatzhöhle," p. 91.

33. Ibid., pp. 35, 33 n. 1, 39, 70. See also Frey, *Diction-
     naire de la Bible, Supplément*, vol. 1, col. 121.

34. Götze, "Die Schatzhöhle," p. 33, n. 1.

35. Götze, *ZSVG* 2 (1924) 51-94.

36. Ibid., p. 94.

37. Z. Avalachvili, *ROC* 26 (1928) 381-405.

38. Ibid., p. 389.

39. See the discussion below, pp. 30-31, 135-36.

40. Avalachvili, *ROC* 26 (1928) 388, 397.

41. S. Grebaut, "Littérature Éthiopienne Pseudo-Clémentine,"
    ROC 6 (1911) 73-84, 167-75, 225-33.

42. A. Dillmann, "Bericht über das Aethiopische Buch Clemen-
    tinischer Schriften," *Nachrichten von der Königliche
    Gesellschaft der Wissenschaften zu Göttingen* (Göttingen,
    1858), pp. 185-226.

43. Grebaut, *ROC* 6 (1911) 73.

44. Ibid., p. 172, n. 6.

45. Frey, *Dictionnaire de la Bible, Supplément*, vol. 1, cols.
    117-25.

46. Ibid., col. 122.

47. Josepheanz, *The Uncanonical Books*, trans. by Issaverdens,
    The Uncanonical Writings.

48. Reinink, *OCA* 197 (1972) 387-99.

49. Reinink seems unaware that Götze had later changed his
    position on this in *ZSVG* 2 (1924) 92-4.

50. Reinink, *OCA* 197 (1972) 391-99.

51. I.e. the cavern itself, not the document named after it.

52. Denis, *Introduction*, pp. 3-14.

53. J. H. Charlesworth, *The Pseudepigrapha and Modern Research*
    (Missoula, Mont.: Scholars Press, 1976), pp. 91-2.

54. G. F. Moore, *Judaism in the First Centuries of the Chris-
    tian Era* (Cambridge: Harvard University Press, 1946;
    repr. ed., New York: Schocken Books, 1971), p. 3. Moore's
    position remains the classic formulation of the monolithic
    view. See also the discussion of Moore's position in
    W. D. Davies, "The Dead Sea Scrolls and Christian Origins,"
    Christian Origins and Judaism (Philadelphia: Westminster
    Press, 1962).

55. Moore, *Judaism*, vol. 1, p. 127.

56. For a discussion of the significance of Jamnia in this
    regard, see W. D. Davies, *The Setting of the Sermon on
    the Mount* (Cambridge: The University Press, 1966), pp.
    256-315.

57. Such considerations as these move G. B. Caird, who calls
     1 Enoch "one of the world's six worst books" (p. 10), to
     the extreme of denying that the Apocalypse of John is
     apocalyptic. G. B. Caird, *The Revelation of St. John the
     Divine* (New York: Harper and Row, Publishers, 1966),
     pp. 10-1.

58. See for example, L. Morris, *Apocalyptic* (Grand Rapids,
     Mich.: Wm. B. Eerdmans Pub. Co., 1972), especially pp.
     73-4, 78-80, 91-2, and 96-101.

59. A. Schweitzer, *The Mysticism of Paul the Apostle* (London:
     A. & C. Black, Ltd. 1931; reprint ed. New York: The
     Seabury Press, 1968), pp. 334-75. See also W. D. Davies,
     Paul and Rabbinic Judaism (London: S.P.C.K. Press, 1948;
     reprint ed. New York: Harper and Row, 1967), pp. vii-
     xvii.

60. G. G. Scholem, *Major Trends in Jewish Mysticism* (New
     York: Schocken Books, 1946; reprint ed. New York:
     Schocken Books, 1974).

61. E. R. Goodenough, *Jewish Symbols in the Greco-Roman
     Period* (New York: Pantheon Books, 1953-68).

62. J. Neusner, "Jewish Use of Pagan Symbols after 70 C.E.,"
     JR 43 (1963) 287.

63. Davies, *Paul and Rabbinic Judaism*, p. 320. It is signifi-
     cant that Davies' landmark work was written before the
     discovery of the Dead Sea Scrolls added their formidable
     weight to his proposals.

64. E. P. Sanders, "The Covenant as a Soteriological Category
     and the Nature of Salvation in Palestinian and Hellenis-
     tic Judaism," in *Jews, Greeks, and Christians*, eds. R.
     Hammerton-Kelly and R. Scroggs (Leiden: E.J. Brill, 1976),
     pp. 11-2.

65. W. F. Albright, "The Dead Sea Scrolls," *AS* 22 (1952/3)
     85, quoted by Davies in *Paul and Rabbinic Judaism*,
     p. xviii.

66. M. Burrows, *The Dead Sea Scrolls* (New York: Viking Press,
     1955), p. 345.

67. Davies, *Paul and Rabbinic Judaism*, p. ix; Davies' intro-
     duction, pp. vii-xv, remains the best summary of the
     shift in scholarly perspective.

68. See the examples marshalled by Davies in *Christian Origins
     and Judaism* (Philadelphia: Westminster Press, 1962),
     p. 219.

69. J. L. Martyn, *History and Theology in the Fourth Gospel*
     (New York: Harper & Row, Publishers, 1968), p. 27.

70. D. R. A. Hare, *The Theme of Jewish Persecution of*

Christians in the Gospel According to St. Matthew
(Cambridge: Cambridge University Press, 1967), pp. 19-77.

71. See the discussion in R. E. Brown, *The Gospel According
to John I-XII* (Garden City: Doubleday and Co., 1966),
pp. lxxiii-lxxv. See also K. L. Carroll, "The Fourth
Gospel and the Exclusion of Christians from the Synagogues," *BJRL* 40 (1957/8) 19-32. For a discussion of the
impact of Jamnia and the imposition of the Birkath ha-
Minim on Christianity see W. D. Davies, *The Setting of
the Sermon on the Mount* (Cambridge: Cambridge University
Press, 1966), especially pp. 275-78.

72. Hare, *The Theme of Jewish Persecution*, p. 79.

73. Ibid., p. 1. Hare further warns here against "over-
simplification" which "reduce(s) the conflict to matters
of orthopraxis as over against orthodoxy."

74. W. A. Meeks, ed., *The Writings of St. Paul* (New York:
W. W. Norton and Co., 1972), p. xiii.

75. The bibliography supporting this point is mountainous.
We cite only two examples: K. Stendahl, ed., *The Scrolls
and the New Testament* (New York: Harper and Brothers,
1957); and J. H. Charlesworth, ed., *John and Qumran*
(London: Geoffrey Chapman, 1972).

76. H. D. Slingerland, *The Testaments of the Twelve Patriarchs: A Critical History of Research* (Missoula, Mont.:
Scholars Press, 1977), pp. 99, 107.

77. R. Reitzenstein, *Das iranische Erlösungsmysterium* (Bonn:
A. Marcus & E. Weber, 1921).

78. In this regard, the contributions of W. Bauer are
extremely valuable. See his *Orthodoxy and Heresy in
Earliest Christianity*, pp. xxi-xxv.

79. E.g. the Turfan fragments from Chinese Turkestan; for a
discussion of this issue see E. Yamauchi, *Pre-Christian
Gnosticism* (Grand Rapids, Mich.: Wm. B. Eerdmans, 1973),
pp. 74-9.

80. See C. Colpe, *Die religionsgeschichtliche Schule: Darstel-
lung und Kritik ihres Bildes vom gnostischen Erlösermythus*
(Göttingen: Vandenhoeck and Ruprecht, 1961), pp. 10-57;
R. N. Frye, "Qumran and Iran: The State of Studies," in
Christianity, Judaism and Other Greco-Roman Cults, ed.
J. Neusner (Leiden: E.J. Brill, 1975), vol. 3, pp. 167-
74; and R. N. Frye, "Reitzenstein and Qumran Revisited
by an Iranian," *HTR* 55 (1962) 261-68.

81. G. MacRae, "The Jewish Background of the Gnostic Sophia
Myth," *NovT* 12 (1970) 98.

82. Ibid., pp. 97-8.

83. R. M. Grant, *Gnosticism and Early Christianity* (New York: Columbia University Press, 1959), p. 41. Grant has since modified his position. See R. M. Grant, "Les etres intermediares dans le Judaisme tardif," in U. Bianchi, *The Origins of Gnosticism: Messina Colloquim*, pp. 141-57, especially pp. 153f.

84. O. Wintermute, "A Study of Gnostic Exegesis of the Old Testament," in *The Use of the Old Testament in the New and Other Essays: Studies in Honor of William Franklin Stinespring*, ed. J. M. Efird (Durham, N.C.: Duke University Press, 1972), p. 256.

85. Ibid., p. 257.

86. Ibid., p. 251.

87. H. Jonas, "Delimitation of the Gnostic Phenomenon--Typological and Historical," in *The Origins of Gnosticism: Colloquium of Messina*, ed. U. Bianchi (SHR 12; Leiden: E.J. Brill, 1967), p. 102. See also R. Haardt, *Gnosis, Character and Testimony*, trans. J. F. Hendry (Leiden: E.J. Brill, 1971), pp. 15-7.

88. See G. MacRae, "The Apocalypse of Adam," *POT*, in press.

89. M. Mansoor, "The Nature of Gnosticism in Qumran," in Bianchi, *The Origins of Gnosticism: Colloquium of Messina*, p. 390.

90. R. H. Charles, *APOT*, vol. 2.

91. J. H. Charlesworth, "Jewish Astrology in the Talmud, Pseudepigrapha, the Dead Sea Scrolls, and Early Palestinian Synagogues," *HTR* (in press). It should be noted that although earlier scholars were aware of the Treatise of Shem, they ignored it because it did not conform to their categories. For an example of the old view with its insistence upon a normative Judaism and its antagonism toward anything astrological, see M. R. Lehmann, "New Light on Astrology in Qumran and the Talmud," *RQ* 32 (1975) 599-602.

92. It appears to have been the influence of the old view which led Renan, Wells and others to attribute the Testament of Adam to the Gnostics, not because of its Gnosticism, but because it could not qualify under their narrow categories as Jewish or Christian.

NOTES TO CHAPTER III

1. See below pp. 102-03.

2. E. Renan, *JA* 5.2 (1853) 427-71.

3. J. P. Migne, *Dictionnaire des Apocryphes* (Paris: Ateliers Catholiques, 1856), vol. 1, cols. 289-98.

4. W. Wright, *Contributions to the Apocryphal Literature of the New Testament* (London: Williams and Norgate, 1865), pp. 61-3. Wright published only the Prophecy of Adam to Seth from ff. 9^b-10^a.

5. M. Kmosko, *PS*, vol. 2, pp. 1309-60. Kmosko's edition utilized MSS A, B, C, D, E, and F.

6. P. Riessler, *Altjüdisches Schrifttum ausserhalb der Bibel* (Heidelberg: F. H. Kerle, 1927; reprint ed. F. H. Kerle, 1966), pp. 1084-90, 1332. Although Riessler does not specify the source of his translation, the appearance of the Hierarchy indicates that it is ultimately taken from Vat Syr 164.

7. Kmosko neglected, either intentionally or through oversight, to include BM Add 15,477 which had been catalogued by W. Wright 36 years earlier; see W. Wright, *Catalogue of Syriac Manuscripts in the British Museum* (London: Gilbert and Rivington, 1871), vol. 2, p. 786. Rylands 44 was unknown to him.

8. Although the dates offered here and below for undated MSS A, G, and H concur with those suggested by W. Wright and A. Mingana, they have been checked by the author against the dated manuscripts found in W. H. P. Hatch, *An Album of Dated Syriac Manuscripts* (Boston: American Academy of Arts and Sciences, 1946).

9. Since the author is restricted to photographs and catalogue entries, A, D, and H are the only MSS whose dimensions he was able to determine.

10. W. Wright, *Catalogue of Syriac Manuscripts*, vol. 2, pp. 781f.

11. J. Assemani, *Bibliothecae Apostolicae Vaticanae Codicum Manuscriptorum Catalogus* (Rome: Typographia Linguorum Orientalium, 1756-59; reprint ed. Paris: Maisonneuve frères, 1927-30).

12. J. Assemani, *Bibliothecae Apostolicae Vaticanae*, vol. 3, pp. 329-31.

13. W. Wright, *Catalogue of Syriac Manuscripts*, vol. 3, pp. 1064-69, especially p. 1066. The Cave of Treasures is located in MS C at ff. 1^a-63^a, and in MS D at ff. 3^b-50^b.

14. W. Wright, *Catalogue of Syriac Manuscripts*, vol. 3, pp. 1207-08; and F. Rosen and J. Forschall, *Catalogus Codicum Manuscriptorum Orientalium qui in Museo Brittanico asservantur* (London, 1838), vol. 1, pp. 95-6.

15. The Syriac text of MS F has been enlarged in the edition below.

16. The references are: M. Kmosko, *PS*, vol. 2, p. 1318, and A. Baumstark, *Geschichte der syrischen Literatur* (Bonn: A. Marcus and E. Weber, 1922), p. 96, n. 1.

17. In a personal letter from Rome dated July 4, 1977, Dr. Richard Rubinkiewicz has kindly informed the author of the correct pagination and that "The error is of . . . a bookbinder which has bound incorrectly all the manuscripts so that no page corresponds now to the ancient pagination."

18. J. Assemani, *Bibliothecae Apostolicae Vaticanae*, vol. 3, pp. 307-19.

19. A. Mingana, "Some Early Judaeo-Christian Documents in the John Rylands Library," *BJRL* (Reprint ed. Manchester: University Press, 1917) 4 (1917) 80.

20. See J. H. Charlesworth, "The Treatise of Shem," *POT* (in press).

21. Wright, *Catalogue of Syriac Manuscripts*, vol. 2, pp. 784-88, especially p. 786.

22. The translation of Budge, *The Cave of Treasures*, pp. 242-48, is taken from the Ethiopic version of the Testament of Adam. The translation by Gibson, *Apocrypha Arabica*, pp. 13-7, is taken from the Arabic.

23. In this regard, see E. J. Epp, "The Eclectic Method in New Testament Textual Criticism: Solution or Symptom," *HTR* 69 (1976) 211-57, especially p. 256.

24. It must be noted here that these libraries, in contrast to some others, have proven in every instance to be responsive and eager to disseminate the materials entrusted to their care.

25. It is more likely in this case that D has excised the hours of the night, than that C has added them, since C is the older of the two manuscripts and since any account of the hours borrowed from recs. 1 or 2 would contain the hours of the day as well as those of the night.

26. As, for example, at 1:1 and 1:2.

27. As, for example, at 1:9, 1:11 and 4:1 (the identification of the fig as the forbidden fruit).

28. For example, D omits all but the Prophecy and C omits the hours of the day. Both omit the section on Bethlehem and the gifts of the Magi in recensions 1 and 3.

29. This generalization would be more significant if the hours of the day lacking in rec. 2 could be compared as well.

30. At 3:3 where Christ will create a new heaven (rec. 1) *and* a new earth (rec. 2).

31. Although even in the Prophecy recs. 2 and 3 often agree against 1.

32. See J. Assemani, et al., eds., *Ephraem Syri Opera omnia quae exstant graeca, syriace, latine, in sex tomos* (Rome: J.M.H. Salvioni, 1737-43), vol. 2, p. 428E. According to Kmosko, in *PS*, vol. 2, p. 1353, n. 1, this passage is also attributed to Ephraem Syrus in *Breviario Ecclesiae Antiochenae Syrorum* (Mosul, 1886), vol. 2, p.ܪܥܚ , col. b, but the author has been unable to verify this reference.

33. MS E begins "From the Book of Splendors, From the First Testament of Our Father Adam"; MS H begins "Concerning the Hours From the Testament of Our Father Adam."

34. M. Kmosko, *PS*, vol. 2, p. 1311, and G. J. Reinink, *OCA* 197 (1972) 391-95, esp. n. 19.

35. See the notes to the translation and below, pp. 157-60.

NOTES TO CHAPTER IV

1. I.e., *talismans*.

2. M. R. James, *Apocrypha Anecdota*, vol. 2, no. 3, pp. 138-45.

3. R. Reitzenstein, *Poimandres* (Leipzig: B.G. Teubner, 1904), p. 258.

4. Nau, *PS*, vol. 2, pp. 1363-81.

5. F. Boll, *Catalogus Codicum Astrologorum Graecorum* (Brussells: Lamertin, 1908), vol. 7, pp. 177-79.

6. A. Delatte, *Anecdota Atheniensia* (Liège: Vaillant-Carmane, 1927), vol. 1, pp. 572-612. The Horarium appears on pp. 601-03.

7. This judgment agrees with that of M. L. Concasty, in *Catalogue des manuscrits grecs, le supplément grec* (Paris: Bibliothèque Nationale, 1960), vol. 3, p. 296. See below pp. 130-31.

8. Cp. folio 169^b (D) with folio 247^b (A).

9. See below pp. 136-37.

10. Cedrenus cites no references, and his account is shorter than any other recension, Greek or Syriac. Since his entire *Compendium* is a collage of information drawn from many sources without any attempt to reproduce those sources exactly, it is possible that the hours of the day have been drawn from the Testament of Adam in a paraphrastic manner.

11. As is indicated by comparing the variants from MSS BCDEF.

12. Bekker, *George Cedrenus*, vol. 1, pp. 17-8.

13. Boll, *Catalogus Codicum Astrologorum Graecorum*, vol. 7, pp. 177-79.

14. Delatte, *Anecdota Atheniensia*, pp. 601-03.

15. Different readings are found at 1:5, 1:9, 1:10b (γέρων), 2:7b (ἅπαν τό). Superior readings are at 1:10a (αἰνοῦσιν), 1:10b (δαιμονοῦντας), 2:2a, 2:7b (ἀλείψει and ἀπαλλαγήσεται), 2:8, and 2:12.

16. At 1:3, 1:4, 1:5, 1:10b (twice), 2:2b, 2:7a, and 2:8.

17. Nau, *PS*, vol. 2, pp. 1370-71.

18. See Delatte, *Anecdota Atheniensia*, p. 446.

19. See K. Preisendanz, *Papyri Graecae Magicae; die griech-
    ischen Zauberpapyri* (Leipzig: Teubner, 1941), vol. 2,
    p. 234 for a list of such names and the texts in which
    they occur.

20. BE share the formula ἐν αὐτῇ τῇ ὥρᾳ against the ἐν ᾗ of
    AD, or the ἐν ταύτῃ ὥρᾳ of C, and the forumula ἡ (πρώτη,
    etc.) ὥρα against ADC ῞Ωρα (α´, etc.). Both also omit the
    eighth hours of the day and night.

21. E.g., the omission of the fifth and tenth hour of the
    night, or the reading ἄγγελοι against ἐκλεκτοί at 1:11.

22. The exceptions being 1:1 and 2:6, where C agrees with BE.

23. E.g., the omission of τὸν θεόν at 1:6; ἔμπροσθεν τοῦ θεοῦ
    at 1:7; the omission of all but the name of the hour at
    1:9, etc.

24. Since the relationship of the Greek and Syriac bears more
    directly on the problem of original language, it will be
    treated more fully below. See pp. 138-41.

25. I.e., at 1:3, 4, 5, 9, and at 2:2, 3 (BCE), 4, 8, and 10.

26. G. W. H. Lampe, *A Patristic Greek Lexicon* (Oxford: Claren-
    don Press, 1961), p. 217.

27. Ibid., p. 1261.

28. Blum, *Eranos* 44 (1946) 317.

29. Ibid., p. 322.

30. Ibid.

31. I.e., Theophanes Continuatus (10th century), Cedrenus (11th
    century), Nicetas Choniates (13th century), Pseudo-Codinus
    (15th century), and our manuscripts (15th to 17th centur-
    ies).

32. See Sophocles, *Greek Lexicon*, pp. 1012-13.

33. See *Webster's Third New International Dictionary of the
    English Language Unabridged* (Springfield, Mass.: G & C
    Merriam Co., Publishers, 1961), s. v. "talisman," p. 2333.

34. James, *Apocrypha Anecdota*, p. 138.

1. This assumes the earliest possible date for Christian documents in Arabic to be the late sixth century. However, a date two hundred years later than this is much more probable. See H. Gibb, *Arabic Literature* (Oxford: Clarendon, 1963), pp. 13, 37-41, 46-51.

2. See Dillmann, *Nachrichten von der Königliche Gesellschaft der Wissenschaften zu Göttingen*, pp. 185-226; Bratke, *ZWT* 1 (1893) 493; and Grebaut, *ROC* 6 (1911) 73.

3. A. Graf, *Geschichte der christlichen arabischen Literatur*, (Studi e Testi 118; Vatican: Bibliotheca Apostolica Vaticana, 1944), p. 200.

4. See below pp. 149-51.

5. See above pp. 30-31.

6. Reinink, *OCA* 197 (1972) 391f. See also James, *Apocrypha Anecdota*, p. 141.

7. This formula consists of the injunction against associating with the children of Cain and the arrangements for care of the patriarchal remains. See Reinink, *OCA* 197 (1972) 392, and Gibson, *Apocrypha Arabica*, pp. 13, 19, 20, 23, etc.

8. Götze, *ZSVG* 2 (1924) 92.

9. See Reinink, *OCA* 197 (1972) 393.

10. See Bratke, *ZWT* 1 (1893) 493; and Grebaut, *ROC* 6 (1911) 73.

11. Avalachivili, *ROC* 26 (1927/8) 384-91.

12. See below p. 153.

13. See above p. 111, n. b.

14. See above p. 123, n. g.

15. See above p. 113, n. e. Note that the Hebrew plurals were adopted in Greek usage and do not of themselves indicate a Hebrew original (see Lampe, *A Patristic Greek Lexicon*, pp. 1230, 1523-24).

16. See Renan, *JA* 5.2 (1853) 461, and Nau, *PS*, vol. 2, p. 1376.

17. Bezold, *Orientalische Studien*, pp. 895, 909.

18. I. Goldziher, "Die Bedeutung der Nachmittagszeit im
     Islam," *AR* 9 (1906) 301.

19. Nau, *PS*, vol. 2, pp. 1363-81.

20. Ibid., p. 1371.

21. Ibid.

22. Ibid., p. 1374.

23. Reinink, *OCA* 197 (1972) 391, n. 19.

24. I.e., Ὧρα β' instead of ἡ δευτέρη ὥρα.

25. Denis, *Introduction*, p. 11.

26. See above pp. 132-33.

27. See for example, Nau, *PS*, vol. 2, p. 1371.

28. See Götze, *ZSVG* 2 (1924) 94.

29. Since serpents obviously do not eat people.

30. The reading of rec. 2 is undoubtedly the original here;
     cf. Gen 1:17 and ApMos 24:1.

31. Compare for example MSS A and B at 3:1, and 3:5 in all
     three recensions.

32. In the Hierarchy, 4:7 reads with the Peshiṭta "which was
     standing among the trees . . . " (. . . ܐܝܠܢܐ ܒܝܬ ܩܡܗ‍),
     while the Septuagint reads "he stood between the two . . .
     mountains" (εἱστήκει ἀνὰ μέσον τῶν δύο ὀρέων . . .).

33. Renan, *JA* 5.2 (1853) 468, n. 19.

34. See below pp. 146-49.

35. Book of the Bee, chap. 5. See E. A. W. Budge, *The Book of
     the Bee* (Anecdota Oxoniensia Semitic Series 1.2; Oxford:
     Clarendon, 1886), pp. 9-11 and Syriac text ad. loc.

36. This angelology omits the rank of ܚܝܠܐ (δυνάμεις) and
     follows the order given in Col 1:16 rather than Eph 1:21.
     No functions are assigned to the various ranks in this list.

37. See Bezold, *Die Schatzhöhle*, vol. 2, Syriac p. 1, and
     Budge, *The Cave of Treasures*, pp. 44-6. For the dates of
     the Syriac Cave of Treasures, see Götze, "Die Schatzhöhle,"
     pp. 90-1.

38. Götze, *ZSVG* 2 (1924) 52.

39. Budge, *The Book of the Bee*, pp. 10-1.

40. These deleted elements include the mention of "David the
     prophet" (4:3), the vision of Zechariah (4:7), the defeat

of Sennacherib and Antiochus (4:6-7), and a vision of
Judah the Maccabee, also alluded to in 2Mac (4:7).

41. Renan, *JA* 5.2 (1853) 427.

42. See, for example Hort, *Dictionary of Christian Biography*,
     p. 37; Frey, *Dictionnaire de la Bible, Supplément*, vol. 1,
     col. 117; and Denis, *Introduction*, p. 10.

43. See the argument above p. 106.

44. E.g. Jub, ApocAd, *Vita*, ApMos, CaveTreas, etc. See also
     Josephus, *Ant*. 1.2.

45. Renan, *JA* 5.2 (1853) 468, n. 19.

46. All of these names are found in the Old and New Testaments.

47. The order in our document and in Eph 1:21 is ἐξουσίαι
     (ܫܘܠܛܢ̈ܐ), δυνάμεις (ܚܝ̈ܠܐ), and κυριότητες (ܡܪ̈ܘܬܐ); that of
     pseudo-Dionysius is ἐξουσίαι, κυριότητες, and δυνάμεις.
     See P. Hendrix, *Pseudo-Dionysii Areopagitae De Caelesti
     Hierarchia* (Textus Minores XXV; Leiden: E.J. Brill, 1959),
     p. 15.

48. Hendrix, *Pseudo-Dionysii Areopagitae*, pp. 14-26.

49. See the argument above pp. 143-44.

50. This list containing the same ranks (omitting δυνάμεις/
     ܚܝ̈ܠܐ) is found in the opening lines of the Cave of Trea-
     sures, but the arrangement follows the order of Col 1:16.
     See Bezold, *Die Schatzhöhle*, vol. 2, Syriac p. 1, and
     Budge, *The Cave of Treasures*, p. 44.

51. As, for example, Kmosko, *PS*, vol. 2., p. 1310.

52. Generally following Renan's judgment in *JA* 5.2 (1853) 434-
     37. See, for example, Leclercq, *Dictionnaire d'archeologie*,
     vol. 1, col. 514, and Migne, *Dictionnaire des apocryphes*,
     vol. 1, cols. 289-90.

53. See above pp. 20-21 and below pp. 154-56.

54. Renan, *JA* 5.2 (1853) 428, 430-31. See also Hort, *Diction-
     ary of Christian Biography*, vol. 1, pp. 37-8.

55. R. Duval, *Anciennes Littératures Chrétiennes* (Paris:
     Librairie Victor Lecoffre, 1907[3]; reprint ed. Amsterdam
     1970) pp. 90-1.

56. Götze, "Die Schatzhöhle," p. 33, especially n. 1, and
     above pp. 25-26. Götze says that the Testament of Adam must
     once have stood in the Cave of Treasures, but goes on to
     say that it could not have been the Testament of Adam known
     from Vat Syr 58 where Adam is buried not in the Cave of
     Treasures but in the city of Enoch. But since all recen-
     sions of the Testament of Adam place Adam's burial by the
     city of Enoch, it could not have been our Testament that
     stood in the Cave of Treasures.

57. Hort, *Dictionary of Christian Biography*, vol. 1, p. 37,
     and Renan, *JA* 5.2 (1853) 428.

58. See B. Altaner, "Zur Frage der Definibilität der Assumptio
     B. M. V.," *TR* 44 (1948) ·135. See also Wright, *Contribu-
     tions to the Apocryphal Literature of the New Testament*,
     p. 7, where Wright argues in the opposite direction that
     the *Transitus Mariae* cannot be earlier than the fourth
     century A.D. because it quotes from the Testament of Adam.

59. See above p. 9 , and F. L. Cross, *The Oxford Dictionary
     of the Christian Church* (Oxford: Oxford University Press,
     1974²), p. 385.

60. A. Smith Lewis, *Apocrypha Syriaca*, p. 41.   ·

61. See W. Wright, "The Departure of My Lady From this World,"
     JSL N.S. 6 (1865) 417-18, 7 (1865) 144-45, and *Contribu-
     tions to the Apocryphal Literature of the New Testament*,
     pp. 7, 24-5. The impression given by I. Ortiz de Urbina
     that the citation from the Testament of Adam is not found
     in the earliest manuscripts of the *Transitus Mariae* is
     incorrect (*Patrologia Syriaca*, [Rome: Pontificum Institutum
     Orientalium Studiorum, 1958], p. 87).

62. F. Stegmüller dates the *Transitus Mariae* in the fourth or
     fifth century A.D., but the Testament of Adam in the sixth
     century A.D. See *Repertorium Biblicum Medii Aevi* (Madrid:
     Graficas Marina, 1940 [i.e. 1950]), vol. 1, pp. 31, 135.

63. From Syriac rec. 2.

64. This translation of 33:1-8 is from O. Wintermute, "The
     Apocalypse of Elijah," *POT* (in press).

65. Note that this conforms well to the date required by M. R.
     James' proposed Latin version of the Testament of Adam.
     See above p. 152.

66. See below pp. 156-58.

67. James, *JTS* 7 (1906) 562-63, and Nau, *PS*, vol. 2, p. 1370.
     See also above pp. 13-14.

68. See Cross, *The Oxford Dictionary of the Christian Church*,
     p. 969.

69. See above pp. 137-39.

70. See above pp. 143-44.

71. See above p. 79 n. a, 146-47.

72. As, for example, pp. 132-33.

73. See above p. 135.

74. See above pp. 132-33.

75. Nau, *PS*, vol. 2, pp. 1363-71.

76. For a fuller discussion of the objections to Nau's thesis, see above pp. 138-41.

77. See above p. 21 n. 10.

78. See Bauer, *Orthodoxy and Heresy in Earliest Christianity*, pp. xxi-xxv, and J. Robinson, ed., *The Nag Hammadi Library*, especially pp. 1-10.

79. See Jonas, "Delimitation of the Gnostic Phenomenon," pp. 90-108, and J. H. Charlesworth, "The Odes of Solomon-- Not Gnostic," *CBQ* 31 (1969) 357-69.

80. Although Frey did find the document bizarre. See *Dictionnaire de la Bible, Supplément*, vol. 1, col. 122.

81. As, for example: sleep and awakening, aeons, archons, incorruptible knowledge, alien, the middle, intoxication, etc.

82. M. Hengel, *Judaism and Hellenism* (Philadelphia: Fortress Press, 1974), vol. 1, pp. 156-57.

83. G. von Rad, *Old Testament Theology* (New York: Harper and Row, Publishers, 1965), vol. 2, p. 100. Also see von Rad's discussion of "the divine determination of times" in *Wisdom in Israel* (Nashville: Abingdon Press, 1972), pp. 263-83.

84. Ginzberg, *The Legends of the Jews*, vol. 5, p. 61.

85. Cp. *Ant.* 1.2.3, ApocAd 69:2-70:9.

86. ApMos 33:1-40:2, *Vita* 45:3-46:1, Jub 4:29, and the Armenian Death of Adam.

87. BR 22.7, PRE 21, Yeb. 62a, Gen.R. 22:2.

88. ApMos 20:4-5 and Gen.R. 15.

89. Jub 4:9.

90. I.e., in 3:1, 3:3, 3:4, and in recs. 1 and 3 only, 3:7b.

91. Col 1:16, Eph 1:21, 1En 14, 2En 20:1, and TLev 3:7-8.

92. The form of the angelology in the Hierarchy is certainly earlier than that found in the thirteenth century account found in the Book of the Bee. See Budge, *The Book of the Bee*, pp. 9-11, and above pp. 143-44.

93. See W. Bousset, "Eine jüdische Gebetssammlung im siebenten Buch der apostolischen Konstitutionen," *Nachrichten von der Koniglichen Gesellschaft der Wissenschaften zu Göttingen*, philol-hist. Klasse (Göttingen, 1915/6), pp. 435-85, and E. R. Goodenough, *By Light, Light* (New Haven: Yale University Press, 1935).

94. From AposCon 7.26.1.

95. From AposCon 7.37.5. The translation of both of these
     passages is taken from D. Darnell, "The Sixteen Synagogal
     Hymns," *POT* (in press).

96. I.e., the references to the defeat of Sennacherib and
     Antiochus, the visions of Zechariah and Judah the Maccabee
     and the "Prophet" David.

SELECTED BIBLIOGRAPHY

Adler, W. "Notes to the Text of George Syncellus and Pseudo-
    Malalas." Paper prepared for the Joint Pseudepigrapha/
    Nag Hammadi Special Session of the Society of Biblical
    Literature, December 1977. (offset printed)

Albright, W. F. "The Dead Sea Scrolls." *American Scholar* 22
    (1952/3) 77-85.

Altaner, B. "Zur Frage der Definibilität der Assumptio B. M. V."
    Theologische Revue 44 (1948) 130-39.

Assemani, J. *Bibliothecae Apostolicae Vaticanae Codicum
    Manuscriptorum Catalogus.* Rome: Typographia Linguorum
    Orientalium, 1756-59; reprint ed. Paris: Maisonneuve
    frères, 1927-30.

_____. *Bibliothecae Orientalis.* Rome, 1725.

Assemani, J., et al., eds. *Ephraem Syri Opera omnia quae exstant
    graece, syriace, latine, in sex tomos.* Rome: J.M.H.
    Salvioni, 1737-43.

Avalachvili, Z. "Notice sur une Version Géorgienne de la
    Caverne des Trésors." *Revue de l'Orient Chrétien* 26 (1928)
    381-405.

Batiffol, P. "Apocalypses apocryphes." *Dictionnaire de la
    Bible.* Paris: Letouzey et Ané, 1895; vol. 1, cols. 764-
    65.

Bauer, W. *Orthodoxy and Heresy in Earliest Christianity.*
    Philadelphia: Fortress Press, 1971.

Baumstark, A. *Geschichte der syrischen Literatur.* Bonn: A.
    Marcus and E. Weber, 1922.

Beer, G. "Pseudepigrapha des Alten Testament." *Realencyclo-
    paedie für protestantische Theologie und Kirche.* Leipzig:
    J.C. Hinrichs, 1905; vol. 16, pp. 263-64.

Bekker, I. *George Cedrenus.* In *Corpus Scriptorum Historiae
    Byzantinae.* Bonn: Weber, 1828; vol. 1.

Bezold, C. "Das arabisch-äthiopische Testamentum Adami."
    *Orientalische Studien Theodor Nöldeke zum siebzigsten
    Geburtstag.* Gieszen: Töpelmann, 1906, pp. 893-912.

_____. *Die Schatzhöhle.* Leipzig: Hinrichs, 1883.

Blum, C.   "The Meaning of στοιχεῖον and its Derivates in the
     Byzantine Age." *Eranos* 44 (1946) 315-25.

Böhlig, A., and Labib, P. *Koptisch-gnostische Apokalypsen aus
     Codex V von Nag Hammadi im Koptischen Museum zu Alt-Kairo.*
     Halle: Martin-Luther-Universität, 1963.

Boll, F. *Catalogus Codicum Astrologorum Graecorum.* Brussells:
     Lamertin, 1908.

Bousset, W.   "Eine jüdische Gebetssammlung im siebenten Buch
     der apostolischen Konstitutionen." *Nachrichten von der
     Königlichen Gesellschaft der Wissenschaften zu Göttingen.*
     Philol.-hist. Klass. Göttingen, 1915/6.

Box, G. H.   "4 Ezra." In *The Apocrypha and Pseudepigrapha of
     the Old Testament.* Edited by R. H. Charles. Oxford:
     Clarendon Press, 1913; vol. 2, pp. 542-624.

Bratke, E.   "Handschriften Überlieferung und Bruchstücke der
     Arabisch-aethiopischen Petrusapokalpyse." *Zeitschrift für
     Wissenschaftliche Theologie* 1 (1893) 454-93.

Brown, R. E.   *The Gospel According to John I-XII.*   Garden City:
     Doubleday and Co., 1966.

Budge, E. A. W. *The Book of the Bee.* Anecdota Oxoniensia
     Semitic Series 1.2. Oxford: Clarendon, 1886.

_____. *The Book of the Cave of Treasures.*   London: Religious
     Tract Society, 1927.

Bulletino di archeologia cristiana. 1877. Pl. 5.

Burn, A. E. *Niceta of Remesiana, His Life and Works.* Cambridge:
     Cambridge University Press, 1905.

Burrows, M. *The Dead Sea Scrolls.* New York: Viking Press,
     1955.

Caird, G. B. *The Revelation of St. John the Divine.* New York:
     Harper and Row, Publishers, 1966.

Cardona, G. R.   "Sur le gnosticisme en Arménie--les livres
     d'Adam." In *The Origins of Gnosticism: Colloquium of
     Messina.* Edited by U. Bianchi. Studies in the History of
     Religion 12. Leiden: E.J. Brill, 1967; pp. 645-48.

Carroll, K. L.   "The Fourth Gospel and the Exclusion of Chris-
     tians from the Synagogues." *Bulletin of the John Rylands
     Library* 40 (1957/8) 19-32.

Charles, R. H.   "The Book of Jubilees." In *The Apocrypha and
     Pseudepigrapha of the Old Testament.* Edited by R. H.
     Charles. Oxford: Clarendon Press, 1913; vol. 2, pp. 1-82.

_____.   "2 Baruch." In *The Apocrypha and Pseudepigrapha of
     the Old Testament.* Edited by R. H. Charles. Oxford:
     Clarendon Press, 1913; vol. 2, pp. 470-526.

Charles, R. H., ed. *The Apocrypha and Pseudepigrapha of the
     Old Testament.* 2 vols. Oxford: Clarendon Press, 1913.

Charlesworth, J. H. "Jewish Astrology in the Talmud, Pseude-
     pigrapha, the Dead Sea Scrolls, and Early Palestinian
     Synagogues." *Harvard Theological Review,* in press.

_____. "The Odes of Solomon--Not Gnostic." *Catholic
     Biblical Quarterly* 31 (1969) 357-69.

_____. *The Pseudepigrapha and Modern Research.* Missoula,
     Mont.: Scholars Press, 1976.

_____. "The Treatise of Shem." In *The Pseudepigrapha of the
     Old Testament.* Edited by J. H. Charlesworth. Garden City:
     Doubleday, in press.

_____, ed. *John and Qumran.* London: Geoffrey Chapman,
     1972.

Clement of Alexandria. *The Instructor.* In *The Ante-Nicene
     Fathers.* Edited by A. Roberts and J. Donaldson. Edinburgh:
     Clark, 1868; revised and reprinted ed., Grand Rapids,
     Mich.: Wm. B. Eerdmans Publishing Co., 1950; vol. 2, pp.
     207-98.

_____. *Miscellanies.* In *The Ante-Nicene Fathers.* Edited
     by A. Roberts and J. Donaldson. Edinburgh: Clark, 1868;
     revised and reprinted ed., Grand Rapids, Mich.: Wm. B.
     Eerdmans Publishing Co., 1950; vol. 2, pp. 299-568.

Clemons, J. "A Checklist of Syriac Manuscripts in the United
     States and Canada." *Orientalia Christiana Periodica* 32
     (1966) 224-251, 478-522.

_____. "Some Additional Information on Syriac Manuscripts
     in the United States." *Orientalia Christiana Analecta*
     197 (1972) 505-08.

_____. "Un supplément américain au 'Syriac Catalogue' de
     Cyril Moss." *L'Orient Syrien* 8 (1963) 469-84.

Cohen, A. *The Babylonian Talmud: Abodah Zarah.* London:
     Soncino, 1935.

Colpe, C. *Die religionsgeschichtliche Schule: Darstellung und
     Kritik ihres Bildes vom gnostischen Erlösermythus.*
     Göttingen: Vandenhoeck and Ruprecht, 1961.

Concasty, M. L. *Catalogue des manuscrits grecs, le supplément
     grec.* Paris: Bibliothèque Nationale, 1960.

Cross, F. L. *The Oxford Dictionary of the Christian Church.*
     Oxford: Oxford University Press, 1974[2].

Dalmata, H. *Alcoran.* Edited by T. Bibliander. Zurich,
     1563, pp. 201-12.

Darnell, D.   "The Sixteen Synagogual Hymns."   In *The Pseude-pigrapha of the Old Testament*.   Edited by J. H. Charles-worth.   Garden City: Doubleday, in press.

Davies, W. D.   *Christian Origins and Judaism*.   Philadelphia: Westminster Press, 1962; Reprint ed., New York: Arno Press, 1973.

_____. *Paul and Rabbinic Judaism*.   London: S.P.C.K. Press, 1948; Reprint ed., New York: Harper and Row, 1967.

_____. *The Setting of the Sermon on the Mount*.   Cambridge: Cambridge University Press, 1966.

Delatte, A.   *Anecdota Atheniensia*.   Liége: Vaillant-Carmanne, 1927.

Denis, A. M.   *Introduction aux Pseudépigraphes Grecs d'ancien Testament*.   Studia in Veteris Testamenti Pseudepigrapha 1.   Leiden: E.J. Brill, 1970.

Dillmann, A.   "Bericht über das Aethiopische Buch Clementin-ischer Schriften." *Nachrichten von der Königliche Gesell-schaft der Wissenschaften zu Göttingen*.   Göttingen: 1858.

_____. *Das Christliche Adambuch des Orients*.   Göttingen: Dietrich, 1853.

Dindorf, G.   *George Syncellus et Nicephorous Cp*.   In *Corpus Scriptorum Historiae Byzantinae*.   Bonn: Weber, 1829; vol. 1.

Duval, R.   *Anciennes Littératures Chrétiennes*.   Paris: Librarie Victor Lecoffre, 1907[3]; Reprint ed., Amsterdam, 1970.

Eliade, M.   *The Myth of the Eternal Return or Cosmos and History*.   Translated by W. R. Trask.   Princeton: Princeton Univer-sity Press, 1974.

Epp, E. J.   "The Eclectic Method in New Testament Textual Cri-ticism: Solution or Symptom." *Harvard Theological Review* 69 (1976) 211-57.

Freedman, H.   *The Babylonian Talmud: Baba Mezia*.   London: Soncino, 1935.

_____. *Midrash Rabbah: Genesis*.   London: Soncino, 1939.

Frey, J. B.   "Adam (Livres apocryphes sous son nom)." *Diction-naire de la Bible, Supplément*.   Paris: Letouzey et Ané, 1928; vol. 1.

Frye, R. N.   "Qumran and Iran: The State of Studies." In *Christianity, Judaism and Other Greco-Roman Cults*.   Edited by J. Neusner.   Leiden: E.J. Brill, 1975.

_____. "Reitzenstein and Qumran Revisited by an Iranian." *Harvard Theological Review* 55 (1962) 261-68.

Gibb, H. *Arabic Literature*. Oxford: Clarendon, 1963.

Gibson, M. D. *Apocrypha Arabica*. Studia Sinaitica 8. London, 1901.

Ginzberg, L. "Adam, Book of." *The Jewish Encyclopedia*. New York: Funk and Wagnalls, 1901; vol. 1, pp. 179-80.

_____. *Legends of the Jews*. Philadelphia: Jewish Publishing Society, 1928.

Goldziher, I. "Die Bedeutung der Nachmittagszeit im Islam." *Archiv für Religionswissenschaft* 9 (1906) 293-302.

Goodenough, E. R. *Jewish Symbols in the Greco-Roman Period*. New York: Pantheon Books, 1953-68.

_____. *By Light, Light*. New Haven: Yale University Press, 1935.

Götze, A. "Die Nachwirkung der Schatzhöhle." *Zeitschrift für Semitistik und verwandte Gebiete* 2 (1924) 51-94.

_____. "Die Schatzhöhle Überlieferungen und Quellen." *Sitzungsberichte der Heidelberger Akademie der Wissenschaften*. Philos.-hist. Klasse. Hiedelberg, 1922.

Graff, G. *Geschichte der christlichen arabischen Literatur*. Studi e Testi 118. Vatican: Biblioteca Apostolica Vaticana, 1944.

Grant, R. M. *Gnosticism and Early Christianity*. New York: Columbia University Press, 1959.

_____. "Les etres intermédiares dans le judaïsme tardif." In *The Origins of Gnosticism: Colloquium of Messina*. Studies in the History of Religion. Edited by U. Bianchi. Leiden: E. J. Brill, 1967.

Grebaut, S. "Littérature Éthiopienne Pseudo-Clémentine." *Revue de l'Orient Chrétien* 6 (1911) 72-84, 167-75, 225-33.

Haardt, R. *Gnosis, Character and Testimony*. Translated by J. F. Hendry. Leiden: E.J. Brill, 1971.

Hare, D. R. A. *The Theme of Jewish Persecution of Christians in the Gospel According to St. Matthew*. Cambridge: Cambridge University Press, 1967.

Hatch, W. H. P. *An Album of Dated Syriac Manuscripts*. Boston: American Academy of Arts and Sciences, 1946.

Hendrix, P. *Pseudo-Dionysii Areopagite De Caelesti Hierarchia*. Textus Minores XXV. Leiden: E.J. Brill, 1959.

Hengel, M. *Judaism and Hellenism*. 2 vols. Philadelphia: Fortress Press, 1974.

Holl, K., ed. *Epiphanius: Ancoratus und Panarion*. Leipzig: J.C. Hinrichs, 1915.

Hort, J. A. "Adam, Books of." In *Dictionary of Christian Biography*. Edited by W. Smith and H. Wace. London: John Murray, 1977; vol. 1, pp. 34-9.

Irenaeus. *Against Heresies*. In *The Ante-Nicene Fathers*. Edited by A. Roberts and J. Donaldson. Edinburgh: Clark, 1868; revised and reprinted ed., Grand Rapids, Mich.: Wm. B. Eerdmans Publishing Co., 1950; vol. 1, pp. 309-567.

James, M. R. "Apocrypha." In *Encyclopedia Biblica*. Edited by T. Cheyne. New York: Macmillan, 1899; vol. 1, col. 253.

_____. *Apocrypha Anecdota*. Texts and Studies 2.2. Edited by J. A. Robinson. Cambridge: Cambridge University Press, 1892.

_____. *Apocrypha Anecdota II*. Texts and Studies 5. Edited by J. A. Robinson. Cambridge: Cambridge University Press, 1897.

_____. *A Fragment of the Apocalypse of Adam in Greek*. Texts and Studies 2.3. Edited by J. A. Robinson. Cambridge: Cambridge University Press, 1892.

_____. *The Lost Apocrypha of the Old Testament*. New York: Macmillan, 1920.

_____. "Notes on Apocrypha." *Journal of Theological Studies* 7 (1906) 562-63.

_____. *The Testament of Abraham*. Texts and Studies 2.2. Edited by J. A. Robinson. Cambridge: Cambridge University Press, 1892.

Jonas, H. "Delimitation of the Gnostic Phenomenon--Typological and Historical." In *The Origins of Gnosticism: Colloquium of Messina*. Studies in the History of Religion. Edited by U. Bianchi. Leiden: E.J. Brill, 1967.

Josepheanz, H. S. *The Uncanonical Books of the Old Testament*. [Armenian] Venice: Library of St. Lazarus, 1896. Translated by J. Issaverdens. *The Uncanonical Writings of the Old Testament*. Venice: Armenian Monastery of St. Lazarus, 1901.

Kmosko, M. "Testamentum Adae." In *Patrologia Syriaca*. Edited by R. Graffin. Paris: Firmin-Didot, 1907; vol. 2, pp. 1309-60.

Lake, K. *The Apostolic Fathers*. Loeb Classical Library. New York: G. P. Putnam's Sons, 1930.

Lampe, G. W. H. *A Patristic Greek Lexicon*. Oxford: Clarendon Press, 1961.

Leclercq, H. *Dictionnaire d'archeologie chrétienne et de liturgie*. Paris: Letouzey et Ané, 1924.

Lehmann, M. R. "New Light on Astrology in Qumran and the Talmud." *Revue de Qumran* 32 (1975) 599-602.

Lehrman, S. M. *Midrash Rabbah: Exodus.* London: Soncino, 1939.

Macdonald, D. "Description of the Semitic Manuscripts in the
    Library of the Hartford Theological Seminary." *Journal
    of the American Oriental Society, Proceedings,* March 1894,
    pp. lxix-lxx.

MacRae, G. "The Apocalypse of Adam." In *The Pseudepigrapha of
    the Old Testament.* Edited by J. H. Charlesworth. Garden
    City: Doubleday, in press.

_____. "The Jewish Background of the Gnostic Sophia Myth."
    Novum Testamentum 12 (1970) 86-101.

MacRae, G. W., and Parrot, D. M. "The Apocalypse of Adam (V,5)."
    In *The Nag Hammadi Library.* Edited by J. M. Robinson.
    San Francisco: Harper & Row, Publishers, 1977; pp. 256-64.

Malan, S. C. *The Book of Adam and Eve.* London: Williams and
    Norgate, 1882.

Mansoor, M. "The Nature of Gnosticism in Qumran." In *The
    Origins of Gnosticism: Colloquium of Messina.* Studies in
    the History of Religion 12. Edited by U. Bianchi. Leiden:
    E.J. Brill, 1967.

Margoliuth, G. *Descriptive List of Syriac and Karshuni Manu-
    scripts in the British Museum Acquired Since 1873.* London:
    Longmans & Co., 1899.

Martyn, J.L. *History and Theology of the Fourth Gospel.* New
    York: Harper & Row, Publishers, 1968.

Meeks, W. A., ed. *The Writings of St. Paul.* New York: W.W.
    Norton and Co., 1972.

Meyer, R. "Adambuch." In *Die Religion im Geschichte und Gegen-
    wart.* Edited by K. Galling, et al. Tübingen: Mohr, 1957;
    vol. 1, col. 91.

Meyer, W. "Vita Adae et Evae." *Abhundlungen der bayerischen
    Akademie der Wissenschaften.* Philos.-philol. Klasse,
    14.3. Munich, 1878.

Migne, J. P. *Dictionnaire des Apocryphes.* Paris: Ateliers
    Catholiques, 1856.

_____, ed. *Patrologia Graeca.* Paris: Garnier, 1894.

Miller, J. "Zur Frage nach der Persönlichkeit des Apollonius
    von Tyana." *Philologus* 51 (1892) 581-84.

Mingana, A. *Catalogue of the Mingana Collection of Manuscripts.*
    3 vols. Cambridge: Heffer & Sons, 1933.

_____. "Some Early Judaeo-Christian Documents in the John
    Rylands Library." *Bulletin of the John Rylands Library*
    4 (1917) 59-118.

Moore, G. F. *Judaism in the First Centuries of the Christian Era*. Cambridge: Harvard University Press, 1946; reprint ed., New York: Schocken Books, 1971.

Morris, L. *Apocalyptic*. Grand Rapids, Mich.: Wm. B. Eerdmans Publishing Co., 1972.

Murray, R. *Symbols of Church and Kingdom*. Cambridge: Cambridge University Press, 1975.

Nau, F. "Apotelesmata Apollonii Tyanensis." In *Patrologia Syriaca*. Edited by R. Graffin. Paris: Firmin-Didot, 1907; vol. 2, pp. 1363-85.

Neusner, J. "Jewish Use of Pagan Symbols after 70 C.E." *Journal of Religion* 43 (1963) 285-94.

Odeberg, H. *3 Enoch or the Hebrew Book of Enoch*. Cambridge: Cambridge University Press, 1928; reprint ed., New York: KTAV, 1973.

Ortiz de Urbina, I. *Patrologia Syriaca*. Rome: Pontificum Institutum Orientalium Studiorum, 1958.

Pearson, J. D. "Oriental Manuscripts in Europe and North America." *Bibliotheca Asiatica*, 1971; vol. 7.

Preisendanz, K. *Papyri Graecae Magicae; die griechischen Zauberpapyri*. Leipzig: Teubner, 1941.

Preuschen, E. *Die apokryphen gnostischen Adamschriften*. Giessen: Ricker, 1900.

Quinn, E. C. *The Quest of Seth for the Oil of Life*. Chicago: University of Chicago Press, 1962.

Reinink, G. J. "Das Problem des Ursprungs des Testamentes Adams." *Orientalia Christiana Analecta* 197 (1972) 387-99.

Reitzenstein, R. *Das iranische Erlösungsmysterium*. Bonn: A. Marcus and E. Weber, 1921.

_____. *Poimandres*. Leipzig: B.G. Teubner, 1904.

Renan, E. "Fragments du livre Gnostique intitulé Apocalypse d'Adam, ou Pénitence d'Adam ou Testament d'Adam." *Journal Asiatique* 5.2 (1853) 427-71.

Reisler, P. *Altjüdisches Schrifttum ausserhalb der Bible*. Heidelberg: F.H. Kerle, 1927; reprint ed., F.H. Kerle, 1966.

Roberts, A. and Donaldson, J., eds. *The Ante-Nicene Fathers*. 10 vols. Edinburgh: Clark, 1868-72; revised and reprinted, Grand Rapids, Mich.: Wm. B. Eerdmans Publishing Co., 1950-52.

Robinson, J., ed. *The Nag Hammadi Library*. San Francisco: Harper & Row, Publishers, 1977.

Rogers, R. "A Catalogue of Manuscripts (Chiefly Oriental) in
     the Library of Haverford College." *Haverford College
     Studies* 4 (1890) 239-50.

Rosen, F., and Forschall, J. *Catalogus Codicum Manuscriptorum
     Orientalium qui in Museo Brittanico asservantur.* London,
     1838.

Sanders, E. P. "The Covenant as a Soteriological Category and
     the Nature of Salvation in Palestinian and Hellenistic
     Judaism." In *Jews, Greeks and Christians.* Edited by R.
     Hammerton-Kelly and R. Scroggs. Leiden: E.J. Brill, 1976.

Scholem, G. G. *Major Trends in Jewish Mysticism.* New York:
     Schocken Books, 1946: reprint ed. New York: Schocken
     Books, 1974.

Schürer, E. *Geschichte des jüdisches Volkes im Zeitalter Jesu
     Christi.* Leipzig, 1901-9.

_____. *A History of the Jewish People in the Time of Jesus
     Christ.* Translated by S. Taylor and P. Christie. Edin-
     burgh: T & T Clark, 1924.

Schweitzer, A. *The Mysticism of Paul the Apostle.* London:
     A & C Black, Ltd., 1931; reprint ed. New York: Seabury
     Press, 1968.

Slingerland, H. D. *The Testaments of the Twelve Patriarchs:
     A Critical History of Research.* Missoula, Mont.: Scholars
     Press, 1977.

Smith Lewis, A. *Apocrypha Syriaca.* Studia Sinaitica 11.
     London: C.J. Clay & Sons, 1902.

Sophocles, E. A. *Greek Lexicon of the Roman and Byzantine
     Periods.* Cambridge: Harvard University Press, 1914.

Stegmüller, F. *Repertorium Biblicum Medii Aevi.* Madrid:
     Graficas Marina, 1940 [i.e. 1950].

Stendahl, K., ed. *The Scrolls and the New Testament.* New York:
     Harper and Bros., 1957.

Stone, M. E. "Adam, Other Books of." *Encyclopedia Judaica,*
     vol. 2, col. 245.

_____. "Armenian Canon Lists III--the Lists of Mechitar
     of Ayrivank (c. 1285 C.E.)." *Harvard Theological Review*
     69 (1976) 283-91.

_____. "The Death of Adam--An Armenian Adam Book." *Harvard
     Theological Review* 59 (1966) 283-91.

Strothmann, R. "Die Schatzhöhle." *Der Islam* 13 (1923) 304-07.

Tischendorf, C. *Apocalypses Apocryphae.* Leipzig, 1866; reprint
     ed. George Olmes Hildesheim, 1966.

von Dobschütz, E. "Das Decretum Gelasianum." *Texte und Unter-schungen* 38 (1912) 338-48.

von Rad, G. *Old Testament Theology*. New York: Harper & Row, Publishers, 1965.

_____. *Wisdom in Israel*. Nashville: Abingdon Press, 1972.

Websters Third New International Dictionary of the English Language Unabridged. Springfield, Mass.: G & C Merriam Co., Publishers, 1961. S.v. "talisman."

Wells, L. S. A. "The Books of Adam and Eve." In *The Apocrypha and Pseudepigrapha of the Old Testament*. Edited by R. H. Charles. Oxford: Clarendon Press, 1913; vol. 2, pp. 123-54.

Wintermute, O. "The Apocalypse of Elijah." In *The Pseudepigrapha of the Old Testament*. Edited by J. H. Charlesworth. Garden City: Doubleday, in press.

_____. "A Study of Gnostic Exegesis of the Old Testament." In *The Use of the Old Testament in the New and Other Essays: Studies in Honor of William Franklin Stinespring*. Edited by J. M. Efird. Durham, N.C.: Duke University Press, 1972; pp. 241-70.

Wright, W. *Catalogue of Syriac Manuscripts in the British Museum*. 3 vols. London: Gilbert and Rivington, 1870-72.

_____. *Contributions to the Apocryphal Literature of the New Testament*. London: Williams and Norgate, 1865.

_____. "The Departure of My Lady From This World." *Journal of Sacred Literature* 6 (1865) 417-48 and 7 (1865) 110-60.

_____. *A Short History of Syriac Literature*. London, 1894; reprint ed. Amsterdam: Philo Press, 1966.

Yamauchi, E. *Pre-Christian Gnosticism*. Grand Rapids, Mich.: Wm. B. Eerdmans, 1973.

Zunz, L. *Göttesdienstliche Vorträge der Jüden*. Berlin: A. Asher, 1832.